SONGS AT THE RIVER'S EDGE

Stories from a Bangladeshi Village

Katy Gardner

Pluto **Press**

LONDON • ANN ARBOR MI

This edition first published 1997 by Pluto Press
345 Archway Road, London N6 5AA

British Library Cataloguing in Publication Data
A catalogue record for this book is available from
the British Library

ISBN 9780745310947 pbk
ISBN 074531094X pbk
ISBN 9780745310954 hbk
ISBN 0745310958 hbk

Library of Congress Cataloging in Publication Data
Gardner, Katy.
Songs at the river's edge: stories from Bangladesh village/
Katy Gardner.
    p.   cm.
ISBN 0–7453–1095–8 (hc)
1. Bangladesh—Fiction.
PR4708.G37566   1997
823—dc21   96–49025
                                                       CIP

Designed and produced for Pluto Press by
Chase Production Services, Chadlington, OX7 3LN
Typeset from disk by Stanford DTP Services, Milton Keynes

Printed on Demand by Antony Rowe Ltd, Eastbourne

Twelve-Month Song

It's the month of December and harvest-time.
In January, we thresh the rice in the cold;
Then February passes, Lover, and all I do is cook and cook.
How much you have made your heart into stone, my friend.
In March, the sun's rays burn us up;
In April, my body turns black.
In May, I just worried and worried over you;
How much you have made your heart into stone, my friend.
In June, there was fresh fruit;
In July, the heavy rains came.
August month passed and I waited and waited by the pond for my
    lover;
How much you have made your heart into stone, my friend.
In the month of September we eat fruit cakes;
In October, the cucumbers sweeten.
Then November month goes by, my love, and I just cried and
    cried:
How much you have made your heart into stone, my love...

Song sung by village women

CONTENTS

Preface   viii

1. September – Arrival   1
2. The Lives that Allah Gives   18
3. Hushnia gets Married   27
4. A Woman's Place   43
5. The Lives that Allah Takes   58
6. Roukea Buys a New Sari   66
7. Stories of the Spirits   74
8. Storms   87
9. Abdullah Seeks a Cure   95
10. Alim Ullah goes to Saudi   109
11. Ambia's Story   126
12. November – Departure   137

Glossary   146

PREFACE

Nearly ten years ago I set out on a journey which was to change my life. Although the initial plane trip covered thousands of miles, it was my movement over an unfamiliar cultural terrain which was to affect me the most. Rather than moving around, I stayed put, and in the process learnt a great deal about the people I was living with, about myself, and – perhaps most importantly – about the negotiable nature of the boundaries between 'them' and myself which at first had appeared so unassailable and which over time increasingly melted away.

The purpose of the trip was to carry out fieldwork for a PhD. in social anthropology which I had embarked upon at the London School of Economics.[1] My decision to work in Bangladesh was an odd mixture of the hopelessly romantic (I had fallen heavily for – South Asia on the hippy trail to Kathmandu a few years previously) and the starkly pragmatic (I failed to get a research visa for India and Bangladesh seemed like a reasonable substitute). As it turned out, I was to have no regrets. Not only is rural Bangladesh, with its endless green rice fields and vast, open skies, one of the most beautiful countries I have visited, but since many families in Sylhet (where I ended up living) have relatives in Britain, it has been possible to continue my relationship with the area without continually having to climb on a plane.

In London I decided that Sylhet would be the most interesting place to work. The vast majority of British Bengalis come from Sylhet, and I hoped to live in one of the many villages which since the beginning of this century have sent men not only to the UK, but all over the world, first as 'lascars' working on ships leaving from Calcutta, and later as labour migrants to Britain, the Gulf, and more recently, the Far East. As well as learn as much as I could about local culture, I

1 This was funded by a grant from the Economic and Social Research Council, for which I am very grateful.

wanted to study the ways in which the village had been affected by overseas migration.

Through a variety of contacts I ended up in the offices of a Sylheti non-governmental organisation and through their help was taken to a small village about three hours away from Sylhet Town, introduced to the people who would eventually become my adoptive family, and a date arranged when I would move in. I have called the village Talukpur, although that is not its real name. Likewise I have changed everyones' names in order to protect them. The villagers knew that I planned to write about them, and in general they had no objections, so long as I hid their true identities.

I lived in Talukpur for fifteen months, following the traditional anthropological method of 'participant observation' (in which the researcher lives in a community, strives to become as integrated as possible with local people, yet also has to keep enough distance to 'observe' and eventually write about them). My research included an initial 'survey' of the village, which involved visiting each household and asking various questions about its composition, loosely structured interviews, which I taped (and upon which some of the following stories are based) and endless questions about every subject I could think of, with which I plagued everyone who had the time and the inclination to talk to me. In true anthropological style I probably learnt most when I was not really 'doing' anything other than sitting around, gossiping, and sharing peoples' lives.

I did not find fieldwork an easy process. Besides small details, such as not properly understanding Bengali for at least the first three or four months, my main problem was that it all seemed so intrusive: walking into peoples' homes (in rural Bangladesh doors are always open) and asking all these personal questions. My uneasiness was compounded by the fact that many people initially thought I was a spy. Since the 1970s many British-based Sylhetis have been in the process of reuniting their families in the UK. This often involves protracted 'cases' with the British immigration authorities who, for political reasons, are keen to limit the numbers of Bangladeshis entering Britain, and are thus apt to turn applications down. During the late 1980s the British High Commission was in the habit of carrying out surprise 'village visits' in which the details of peoples' applications were checked, and so, as I had been asking 'when did you last see your father?' type questions, assumptions that I must be working for the British High

Commission were entirely understandable. Only after I had been living in Talukpur for many months did peoples' suspicions begin to decrease; even today, there are probably some people who believe that despite all my baloney about 'writing a book for my studies' I was in fact a spy.

Whilst these were very real, practical difficulties, my paranoia over what people believed me to be doing was related to a wider concern, which no doubt dogs most northern anthropologists working with people from less powerful societies in the south. That 'we' should be able to study and represent 'them' is clearly the direct result of gross global inequalities (these should not, however, be overstated; several households in Talukpur were far wealthier than I was, owning property and businesses in Britain as well as Bangladesh).

One solution to these problems is for people to research their 'own' societies, thus partly (but not wholly) releasing them from the power relations implicit in work such as mine. Whilst working 'at home' is an important corrective, the danger is that anthropological endeavour becomes increasingly inwards looking and cross-cultural comparison obsolete. What is also needed to help redress the balance is, I think, for researchers from places such as Bangladesh to study communities in places such as Britain. As yet this is rare: let us hope that slowly it becomes less so.

Despite my qualms I am glad that I persevered with my fieldwork, for I am convinced that anthropological research is vital for our under-standing of each other. It is, however, a highly subjective art, for knowledge is generated and validated through individual experience, producing narratives which may say almost as much about their writers as they do about the groups they supposedly represent. This is not nec-essarily a problem, so long as anthropological authors admit both to their privileged positions and their subjectivity, to the way in which their own stories have become interwoven with those of the people they are describing.

Locating the author within the text, and attempting to indicate to some extent the subjective nature of ethnography is common practice for most anthropologists working today.[2] What follows is not an academic anthropological text but a series of stories, some of which I

2 See for example my own ethnographic account of Talukpur, and the cultural importance of overseas migration to it in *Global Migrants, Local lives: travel and trans-formation in rural Bangladesh* (Oxford University Press, 1995)

wrote whilst wiling away the evenings in Talukpur, and others which were completed on my return to Britain. Although 'true' in the sense that in essence all the events which I narrate took place, these events have been processed through the filter of my imagination, and have had to fit into my way of telling. The people of Talukpur would, no doubt, tell things in quite a different way.

Since leaving Talukpur in the winter of 1988 I have returned to Sylhet many times. Many things have changed. The family I lived with have largely relocated to the nearby town, and the widowed aunt who lived next door has migrated with her sons to America, leaving their homestead occupied by poorer relatives.

The village is different too. Most of the more prosperous houses are now made with bricks, there is a tarmac road across the fields to the river crossing, and over the last few years electricity has arrived. The last letter I had from Bangladesh told me that one of the brothers of my family has recently started a phone business: the number of his mobile phone, on which he can be contacted in Talukpur, was included. Like most people, those living in Talukpur are continually striving to get ahead and improve their lives; rather than being stuck in some isolated and 'traditional' rural groove, they are very much tied to the ever-changing and ever-dynamic forces which shape the rest of the world. I dedicate the stories that follow to them, for letting me share their lives for a while and for giving me so much more than I could ever give them.

Katy Gardner,
Brighton, 1997

1 SEPTEMBER – ARRIVAL

I arrived in Talukpur one September night, as crickets chanted and jackals screeched to each other across the fields. The moon had already risen high and bright over the still water, and the lanterns had been lit for hours: we had been expected before sunset, but we were late.

We had left Sylhet Town, in the north-east of Bangladesh, early that afternoon. We were a curious party – a middle-aged man with smart town trousers and an officious-looking briefcase with nothing in it but a newspaper; an elderly lady with a missing front tooth and kindly eyes, buttoned up in her all-concealing *burqua* (long cape with veil) and clutching a small packet of *betal* nut and *pan* leaves for the journey; and one over-tall, over-shabbily dressed foreigner with a sweaty face and strange Western jewellery. This stranger obviously had no idea of how to carry on: she did not even have the grace to shield herself from the astounded stares of passers-by with her mud-splattered brolly.

I had met Mustak, my escort, through a local development organisation, and it was to his village that we were going. He was a liberal, who had read widely and educated himself far beyond the usual boundaries of the village. Now he worked and lived in the town, with his young wife and children. Because of this, perhaps, he had hardly batted an eyelid at my professed desire to 'live in a village for a year', and with great efficiency he arranged somewhere for me to stay. The old woman was his distantly related aunt. She clutched my hand and blinked at me in a friendly way as we jolted through the chaos of Sylhet traffic, hunched up together under the rickety canopy of the rickshaw. I understood that she was a close relative of the family with whom I was to live, that her name was Kudi Bibi, and that was about all.

It was the first rural night I had seen. The journey from Sylhet Town to Talukpur, the village where we were going, took about five hours,

and by the time the road ran out, and Mustak had found a boatman
to punt us across the flooded fields, the day was already fading. We
drifted all afternoon through the flat green Bangladeshi countryside
which spreads out endlessly until it meets the enormous sky with its
vast blueness and billowing clouds. The river pulled us for hours
through the scattered villages which lined its bank; past endless
homesteads, with their scattered buildings and yards and their hayricks
spilling into the water; past women washing pots, and listless cattle
which chewed their suppers and looked stupidly across at us. Rows
of waddling ducks quacked uproariously at the sight of the boat. On
and on we went, until the water turned inky and the sky was suddenly
filled with swooping bats and the flicker of glow-moths. Bangladesh
is never still, and nights are never quiet. Instead, the countryside roars
with life: a million insects singing in the dark, and a million human
voices calling and muttering and yawning and praying as the lamps
are lit. As the boat splashed and creaked through the water we passed
others, sometimes containing solitary silent women with their veils
down and their faces turned away, but more often workmen in their
bamboo hats singing at the tops of their voices about lost love or the
greatness of their saints, as they disappeared almost completely into
the dark. All along the horizon were continual flashes of electricity
and the distant rumble of thunder, even though the sky was clear.

After seemingly endless turns in the river, our decrepit wooden boat
glided round a corner, and then at last I was told: 'That's it! We're
here ...'

The boat turned towards a clump of trees. Within them was what
would be my home for the next fifteen months. We slowly approached
the land of the *bari* (homestead), which in this, the wet season, had
become an island in the monsoon waters. I could glimpse buildings
through the greenery; there was no sign of light or, for that matter,
life. But then with a crash a door swung open, and a lantern appeared.
I could hear excited voices shouting out to each other, and see figures
hurrying towards us.

The boat struck land with a jolt. The figures now had faces, and
were growing into a crowd. For a moment I sat in the boat clasping
my bags and facing the people as they came nearer. More than
anything, I wanted to turn round and go home. In that short second,
I was terrified. And likewise, the people coming towards me must have

had their fears: they had volunteered their hospitality to me, but they did not know what problems I, a young woman from the West, might bring them. If I was scared by their unfamiliarity so, no doubt, were they by mine.

So we stood momentarily facing each other, on two sides of a cultural divide that I was hoping would not last.

Then the moment ended and the silence was burst with a babble of words. My bags were taken from me by a gaggle of small boys, and numerous hands helped me step out of the narrow boat. An old man stood apart from the crowd, smiling humorously and shouting directions at the boatman. Several girls grinned shyly and giggled when I tried to say the Islamic greeting: '*Salaam-e-lekum*'. A rounded, pretty woman with a worn face and broken spectacles took me firmly by the arm and guided me through the slippery dark yard towards the buildings. I thought I heard the word '*Amma*' (Mother) – but maybe not. Friendly voices told me things and asked me questions, none of which I understood. With a practised hand, another woman pulled the *orna* (long scarf) I was wearing across my chest, up, and over my head. Everyone laughed. It was the first small gesture in a long process of helping me to become like them. The material felt uncomfortable over my hair, but I tried to stop it from falling off.

This was really it, then. I had arrived.

Arrivals are nothing special in Talukpur, for these days they happen all the time. As the villagers found themselves part of Pakistan, and then suddenly part of the newly created Bangladesh, their community expanded and events in the outside world increasingly intruded into their lives. A war of independence was fought, and in Dhaka presidents came and went. The infant Bangladesh lurched from hope, to coup, to famine; to more coups, cyclones and floods. People stopped being so optimistic, and began to plan ways of escaping from the poverty which so often surrounded them. Back in Talukpur, too, villagers looked beyond their own small patch for their futures. For several generations there had been a tradition of young men travelling to Calcutta to find work on ships which took them all over the world. Many had stayed on in Britain and America, coming home only for brief trips before returning for more work in the factories and restaurants which were helping to make some of them rich back in their villages. Now, the trickle became a steady flow. In the 1960s the British government encouraged men from Commonwealth countries all over the world to provide a cheap labour force for its expanding domestic economy, and thousands of men from Talukpur, and the other villages around it, left for the industrial cities of Britain. Others went to the Middle East to work on building sites, or as street vendors, or in all manner of jobs which they did not talk about when they got home. Their wages helped their families to get by.

So over the years the village had been tied to the outside world by many fine threads which wrapped their way around it, and pulled it with them. On the surface, nothing had changed very much. The rice was planted each season, and after it had turned from bright green to the gold of harvest time, teams of scraggy bulls were used to plough the land. The rains came, and as the fields filled with water the men would spend their days fishing from them, bringing home pots filled with shrimps and fish. Women still hid from strangers and in public usually covered their faces with veils; marriages were largely still arranged and the rulings of the elders held. But these days, too, paths had been built, and big launches carried passengers from the local villages towards the road. People could move more easily around the countryside. More of them had travelled on buses or in cars, more had visited Sylhet, and more could read and write. Talukpur still had no tarred road or electricity, but as the accoutrements of the modern world edged slowly closer, as year by year the lines and bridges were extended, everyone was well aware that, Allah willing, they were coming. Arrivals, then, be they of new ideas, new goods, or new people, were not really anything special.

As for me, I was to make the journey to the village many times, although never in such style as that first September night. As the waters receded and the paths dried out, I discovered that I could walk the five miles from the road across the fields, and – give or take the perils of the odd bamboo bridge (one pole to walk along, with another usually extremely rickety one at an angle to cling on to) – get home with far more ease than in a cramped and soggy boat. Best of all was during the driest part of the dry season, when I could take a rickshaw right into the village. This was ideal, for as time wore on and I became more versed in local attitudes, and aware of how outrageous my behaviour was, I developed a dread of walking alone. I hated being stared at as I passed through villages which lay on the path to Talukpur, and loathed hearing the snatches of excited conversation which rose up in small gusts whenever I appeared:

'Who *is* she?'

'Where's she going?'

'Look, she's alone!'

'Hey, *Beti* [lass], is there no one with you?'

The worst option was to take the launch from the river a few miles away to the Dhaka road, ten miles down river. To get on the boat involved jostling over planks perched precariously above thick, fetid sewage, and then cramming myself into the women's cabin, which was invariably filled to bursting with hot women chewing betel, and children sucking at ice-lollies or vomiting over their mothers' saris. I could never sit in that cabin and not curse the men. That *they* had a vast cabin to themselves on that launch, and had condoned the rules which meant that we women were herded together like cattle to avoid the shame of being seen by *them*, made me want to spit. The flexibility to different people's customs, which I had never found difficult when travelling through a country, soon disintegrated after staying put in Bangladesh for more than a couple of months, and never was I more of a cultural bigot than when I was sitting on that launch. I am ashamed to say that at those times, when men bunched around the open doorway of the women's cabin to gawp at me – deciding, no doubt, that since I was alone and Western I must be fair game – I forgot all about cultural relativity and tolerance. The groups who peered and whispered and giggled at me often became the astounded objects of my wrath, stunted and badly expressed as it was:

'What are you staring at? Don't you have any shame? Go away! I don't like this at all!' I was apt to cry when my patience ran out altogether.

When I eventually arrived in Talukpur I would recount these exchanges to the women in my family, who would hoot with laughter and then say: 'But you can do this. We could never say such things ...'

Talukpur was a very typical village, if there is such a thing. It was surrounded by fields, and divided by a small river which ran through it. In the dry season this turned into pasture-land; in the monsoon it swelled with water and carried great cargo boats laden with bricks or clay pots, sailing boats, and small private boats with bamboo cabins through the village. At one end were a few tea-stalls and 'tailor shops', which were actually just stalls where men sat hopefully with sewing machines. There was a mosque and a *madrasa*, where a small group of young men learnt to recite the *Qur'an*. Most of the villagers were Muslim, but not all. At the edge of the cluster of homesteads, and beyond the tea-stalls, was a large gathering of mud-and-straw buildings. This was the bari of the village Hindus, all of whom were members of the fisherman *Patni* caste. About two miles away, nearer the Kustia River, was a large bazaar where the men shopped for things which the village did not produce itself. At lean times of the year some families even had to buy in extra rice. It was perhaps smaller than some villages, and certainly the area was richer than most other parts of Bangladesh, but there was nothing so very special about it.

The family led me inside the buildings of their homestead. Unlike the poorer houses of most of rural Bangladesh, their home had been built with sturdy concrete, and ornate flowers and an inscription in Arabic had been painted on its front. Although my newly adopted family owned only an average amount of land, they had relatives abroad, and many years ago the earnings sent to them from Britain had been spent on the new house. But despite the solid walls and ostentatious appearance of the bari, inside it the floors were made of packed earth, and the walls were bamboo.

We went through the main part of the building where the men slept and the grain was stored, and into the small room where I was to live. I knew how lucky I was to have so much space to myself – everyone else slept five to a bed, or more. But the beds were huge, and as I was told many times, sleeping alone is a scary and unhappy situation: my solitude was not envied. In the flickering lamplight I could make out my own hulking wooden bed, which took up most of the space, a table and a wooden clothes-stand. It was perfect.

With great hilarity my possessions were unpacked and examined, which at least gave us all something to do and to laugh about. The things I had bought in Sylhet – a hurricane lamp and a mosquito net – were closely examined and put away. Then the table in my room was laid for me to eat, and enormous bowls of rice and fried fish, vegetables and mutton curry, were placed on it. The food was delicious. Although as I settled in such lavish meals were no longer provided in my honour, and I ate normal meals with the family, my appetite for village food never waned.

Lastly, I was taken down to the pond by a small group of giggling children for a wash underneath the stars, and then locked into my tiny little room, with reassurances that this way, with the wooden slats of the window tightly closed and the door barricaded, the night bandits (whom everyone feared greatly, but who never appeared) would have slightly less chance of getting at me. I was exhausted from the long journey, but my mind was buzzing with excitement. I changed into the longest, and thus most respectable nightdress that I had been able to find in Dhaka, and climbed into bed and under my mosquito net. Within two minutes I decided that I would probably suffocate, but when I stuck my head outside for air, the mosquitoes descended with glee. Sweat was dripping from my back and it had begun to rain once more. I could hear the slow mumbles of my newly adopted father's prayers and sleepy female voices from the kitchen area. It was my first night in Talukpur, the start of a different life and a brand-new beginning.

I was woken the next morning at four-thirty by the distant sound of the *azan* (call to prayer) and *Abba* (Father), who had taken his cue from the cries across the fields and was mumbling his prayers. It was barely light outside, but the crickets had stopped chirping and a cock began to crow. A gleam of pink light appeared over the tree tops which surrounded my room. I could hear doors bang and people hawk as they greeted the day with a globule of spit.

I was more than slightly nervous at the prospect of my first day in the village. I knew I would be showered with attention, and would probably be alone only when I went to the latrine. As it turned out, I was accompanied even there. Huge crowds would gather wherever I went and I would be the object of close scrutiny and comment for months. I steeled myself, and climbed out of my mosquito net.

I had come to Talukpur to learn, and the villagers were to be my teachers. After the end of that first day it was obvious to everyone that we had a lot of work to do. With me, they were going to have to start with the basics.

'You're just like a baby,' one of the family sisters said that evening. I was pleased to have understood what she'd said, a rare occurrence in that first week, but not quite so flattered at the content of her words. First, I had to try and sort out just who was who in my adoptive family.

Luckily for me, the bari had only two households; some in the village had as many as nine, the members of which would probably have taken me light years to untangle. Even these two, though, confused me for days, especially the task of sorting out just which children and babies belonged to whom. Head of our household in practice, if not in name, was Amma, a wonderful woman with a proud nose and mouth, sturdy arms, and black bushy hair tied in a knot at her neck. This was cut short to keep her head from overheating, a dangerous condition associated with sickness and mental problems. Although she would have laughed at the notion, Amma was beautiful. She had a large, soft, extremely strong body which had borne twelve children, and strong, wise eyes which had seen four of them die. She padded around the bari tending her vegetable plots, cooking, making mats, fans, clay *hookahs*, and whatever else was needed, and generally being the pillar of the family. Throughout my stay she would regularly come to me and sigh heavily, declaring how terrible everything was: how they couldn't give me good food; how they were so poor; and how she spent every minute of her days worrying over me and praying for my comfort. I soon learnt the appropriate answers to these little speeches and realised that they were her way of showing affection, and I was not meant to take them entirely seriously.

Then there was Abba, who spent his days surveying his fields and saying his prayers. Abba must have been about sixty. He was apt to wander into my room and tell me the names of the British royal family or instruct me on the mistakes which Christian doctrine made compared to the truthfulness of Islam, shake his head, declare 'You'll never understand' and then disappear back to his hookah. Every afternoon he changed into his best *lungi* and punjabi shirt and, with strict instructions from the women on what to buy, set off with his walking stick to the bazaar, a short walk of about two miles across the fields.

There were four daughters, and with the comings and goings of the elder married ones and their children, the household was in constant flux. One of them, Minera, lived in the bari next door. She was married to her cousin, and because she was so close she spent much of her time with us. Another, Saleya, had come back from her husband's village several miles down river to give birth to her fifth child. Then there were Najma and Bebi, the two unmarried daughters, still at home although their school days were long over. Najma had been educated up to class ten, a rare achievement for a village girl, and acted as teacher for the bari children outside the short and irregular hours of the small village school. Her lessons consisted of standing over her small brothers and cousins with a stick, whilst they recited from their books. Not surprisingly, these lessons often ended in noisy tears. Bebi was learning to cook under the keen eyes of her mother and elder sisters in preparation for her eventual marriage, and spent from dawn until long into the night bent over the clay fire, hauling around huge pots of rice and curries, and serving the family their endless meals.

Besides this immediate nucleus of family, there were many more people in the homestead for me to meet. There was a widowed aunt, who lived alone with her children in adjoining rooms. Compared to the lively sociability of our household, hers was quiet and subdued. It was several weeks before we talked together and I was invited to drink tea with her, perching on a floor-stool in her kitchen and looking out at the pond. She had two sallow and silent adolescent sons who, I learnt later, had been instructed not to talk to me in case it compromised my modesty. These young men were rarely present but spent most of their time in the bazaar, posing in Western T-shirts and dark glasses, and listening to loud Bengali pop music.

Then there were numerous little brothers, cousins, and nephews and nieces, who very slowly came into focus until I could eventually put a name to every face. At first they were shy with me, and ran away giggling whenever I spoke to them. This was not to last. As the weeks and months progressed, the children's fear changed to boisterous delight at my strange ways. I was constantly trailed by various small members of the family who loved watching me write and would visit me in my room in little deputations asking to see, just one more time, how my alarm clock worked. When everyone was around there were about twenty-five people on the bari; crammed into five rooms.

There was one more person in those first few days who became increasingly familiar, and whose pretty, smiling face I began to search for whenever I arrived back in the bari after visiting another homestead. This was Sufia, a young woman who came from a homestead just a few minutes' walk away over the fields. She was my new sisters' cousin and often spent her days in our household, helping Amma and Bebi with the cooking and playing with the smallest of the children. Najma and Bebi treated her almost like a sister. She lived, I soon learnt, with the kindly old Kudi Bibi, her aunt. Her parents had both died when she was tiny, Amma told me, sighing, and Kudi Bibi had always brought her up as her own. She was married, but one month after her wedding her husband, like so many other young men in the area, had gone off to work in Kuwait. That had been two years ago, and by the time I left she still had no idea when he would return. In a sense, Sufia did not really belong anywhere, and perhaps that is one reason why she was to become my closest friend. We calculated that she was probably about my age, which meant that neither of us need call the other 'Elder Sister' and behave with the deference and respect which the label involved. I usually spent my evenings with her sitting at the *ghat*, the stone seats and steps leading down to the pond, looking up at the moon while we listened to the young madrasa student who lodged with the family reciting Islamic verses. She was deeply religious and would spend long hours sitting over the Qur'an and whispering the holy words of Arabic which were so important to her, but which she would never understand. Then the time would come for her prayers and one of my young brothers would chaperone her back across the fields to her bari.

My first days were filled with major challenges. One of these was how to wash in the bari pond – or rather, small lake, filled with water hyacinths – without revealing an inch of my forbidden flesh. Village women have this down to a fine art. They can wash in their saris, immerse themselves in the water, rinse off the soap, and then change into a clean blouse, petticoat and sari in about three minutes flat if need be – all without exposing a thing. I was not quite so skilful. I tried at first to bathe in my long nightdress and then change out of the dripping things in the privacy of my room, but this was met with cries of censure. It *was* thin, I confess, and I probably ended up looking more like an entrant for a wet-T-shirt competition than a respectable girl in Muslim Bangladesh. Eventually I learnt how to wriggle out of my clothing under the cover of dry things, but never to anyone's satisfaction. The comment which was to dog me for many months was: 'Ya Allah, girl, don't you have any shame?'

Then I had to learn how to dress properly. I had thought that the *shalwar kameez* sets (baggy trousers and long top) which I had brought with me from Dhaka would be totally acceptable. At first, no one told me to the contrary. But after a few days, when the family women realised that treating me as a high-status dignitary was not perhaps quite the right way to proceed, they became freer in their personal comments and let me know that my style of dress was not really to their taste. Such clothes were for young unmarried girls, not old spinsters like me. I had moved into Talukpur on my twenty-third birthday, and thus by village standards should have been married many years earlier. It was not just they who disapproved; one of the questions which everyone always asked when they first met me was 'Why aren't you wearing a sari?' Eventually I was taken in hand and dressed in Sufia's best nylon sari and high-heeled sandals. To put in bluntly, I felt ridiculous. I couldn't walk without getting the material stuck between my legs, and looked oversized and awkward. The material kept riding up and showing my ankles because I was too tall, and the blouse pinched my arms. But we decided to persevere, and after a week or so of being broken in I eventually took to it, and learnt to love my sari.

Almost every bit of me that wasn't covered up (and some bits that were) came under close scrutiny whenever I met new people, and in my first month in Talukpur, that was every day. After a while I became so familiar with the routine that I had my answers pat. My hands would be taken and squeezed to see how soft they were and whether I'd ever done a day's work. One old man studied my palms closely and declared that I'd have at least ten babies. The saris, bangles and earrings I wore were closely examined. The one question always asked was 'How much was it?' so that I developed such a keen memory for prices that eventually I could recite how much every single thing I owned had cost, and where I had bought it.

My hair was fingered and played with. It did not go down well. In Bangladesh anything other than deep black is associated with poverty, for malnourishment tinges dark hair dull red. My hair is fairish brown, but people called it red, shook their heads sadly and asked me why I didn't use 'Cinderella Hair Darkener' which, according to the packet, not only dyes hair black, but also 'Cools the head and causes sound sleep ... Use Cinderella Hair Darkener and you will not be disgusted by your hair.' I did not feel particularly disgusted by my hair, so I decided to give Cinderella Hair Darkener a miss, but did put oil on it, which pleased everyone because it made it appear darker. One year later, after it had actually become far fairer, people insisted on telling me how black it was – the result, they assured me, of staying in the village for so long.

My skin colour, however, got a better reception. To many village people 'black' is ugly, and 'white' beautiful. This drove me to distraction. Again and again women would squeeze my arm and say, 'You're white. So lovely. Look at me, ugh, black and ugly.' Many of the women were actually stunningly beautiful by Western standards, but try as I might to persuade them, they remained unconvinced. Six months later, by which time my skin had turned brown, everyone was most upset at how my colour had been ruined and my looks destroyed by life in the village.

After a while I grew used to this onslaught of personal comments – but not completely. At first, before I had adjusted to the village diet, which is oily, sugary, and without much vitamin C, I became very spotty. Nobody likes to have spots, but it is even worse when everyone talks about them continuously. An inevitable question in every conversation with me was, 'Yssh! What's all this? It's terrible, she's been ruined by coming here. Don't you have any medicine?'

This was not offensive to anyone but me, and no one ever understood why I always snapped, 'Nothing! Mosquito bites!'

I might add, however, that after a while, perhaps in a strange and totally ineffectual form of revenge, I too was crying, 'Yssh! What's all this?' whenever I spied a blemish on the usually clear skins of the people I knew.

I soon learnt that privacy, our British obsession, counts for very little in Bangladesh. People simply do not understand why anyone should want to be alone. I considered myself very lucky because I had my own room, but to most people this was a definite sign of my oddness and masculinity. 'Aren't you afraid to sleep alone?' they'd ask me.

I always felt vaguely guilty when I shut myself in my room to work or just switch off, but such feelings never lasted long, for whilst I was still a novelty I was almost always joined by people within about five minutes. Everyone was intensely interested in my possessions, which were gone through daily by my visitors. 'What's this?' someone would ask, holding up a stick of deodorant or a hairbrush. Some things I was not willing to explain. I kept my supply of tampons, I had thought, safely hidden. Not so. 'Don't you have any more of that cotton wool for my face?' a sister asked me one day. I looked at her blankly. Cotton wool was not something I had thought vital for village life. I shook my head and she looked at me in sorry disbelief. Later on I discovered little mounds of cotton wool, with telltale blue strings hanging from them, stored carefully with the girls' bottles of hair oil, powder, and plastic bangles.

But perhaps most bewildering for me were the number of new rules I faced. I sometimes felt in those first months that I was walking over a minefield because of all the truly horrifying things I might do without realising it. Suddenly all the definitions of polite social exchange I was used to had changed: I was playing the same game, but with different regulations. Behaviour which might raise British eyebrows – such as asking someone who has just been introduced why they have spots, how much they earn, or why on earth they're not yet married – was suddenly quite acceptable. Likewise, it was normal to enjoy someone's hospitality without once saying 'please' or 'thank you'; whenever I tried to use these words, my hosts laughed aloud at my gauche inappropriateness. To burp and spit was now fine, but to eat with my left hand or go around without an orna definitely was not. There were now so many 'don'ts' that I began to feel like a wild savage. And far more disconcertingly, those 'don'ts' were of a quite different order. Whereas back home breaking the rules merely implied oafishness, here it made one sinful and liable to attack from evil spirits. I sat in doorways, which was offensive to Allah, and a sin; touched the family Qur'an, which was even worse, since I had not first been ritually cleansed; and once came into the building wet, which destroys the power of any amulets (protective charms made of tiny fragments of paper with Qur'anic verse written on them) inside the walls. And then there were all the taboos affecting women, and their state of *sharom* (modesty, shame).

'Sharom' is one of the main explanations which village women give for their actions. A woman who doesn't feel shame is outside society – in fact she is hardly a woman at all (unless she happens to be the English girl, who isn't really female anyway), or at least not one with whom anyone would like to associate. In Britain I had read everything I could lay my hands on about Bangladeshi society and Islam, and naively thought I had a rough idea of how to behave politely, but I still made some terrible blunders. I asked women who were blatantly pregnant when their babies were due, I asked Amma if she shaved her amazingly smooth legs, and I asked young women whether or not they were married. All these questions, put by a stranger, result in their victim covering her face with her sari and making a hasty exit. Later on, when

I had learnt the hushed and sufficiently conspiratorial tone of voice to use, and people had begun to trust me, I could ask almost anything.

In a way, harder than learning what were no-go areas for the people whose lives I was trying to understand was readjusting my own personal taboos. Everything was reversed. Whilst villagers were squeamish about discussing marriage and sexual matters, they were quite at ease with lavatorial concerns. Indeed, they were happy to discuss them in the greatest of detail. The latrine in our bari did not have a door, but a rotted bamboo mat acting as a screen which one squatted behind, so that if anyone appeared, all would be revealed. During the monsoon this mat rapidly deteriorated until it was more hole than bamboo, but nobody considered mending it. At night the bari women relieved themselves together for fear of evil spirits, an activity which I admired, but was always too shy to join.

Along with this communality and openness, people did not have the slightest hesitation in discussing their bowel movements – or mine, for that matter. In the first week of my stay, desperately con-stipated after being fed nothing but white rice and curry and engulfed in my own very English version of shame, I asked Abba to bring me some laxatives from the bazaar. This whispered request led to a loud family conference over the state of my 'unopened' stomach, and what to do about it. Later the village Chairman, on a visit, was also included in the discussion.

People's attitudes towards dirt were also very different from mine. The boundary between house and outside is far more blurred in Bangladeshi villages than in the West. Most floors in Talukpur are made of earth (as are the walls of many of the houses: others are made of bamboo) and no one bothers with netting or glass in the windows. The insides of buildings are used for storing grain and farming tools and housing the ducks, hens and goats, as well as humans. It is impossible to shut out nature, even if one particularly wanted to. There are always lizards and rats and frogs to keep one company, plus a variety of other beasties towards which I remained rather less than friendly. Household cleanliness was more than a little different from what I was used to. Babies, of course, don't wear nappies, and no one minds if they shit or pee on the floor. Eventually, maybe some hours later, someone covers up the mess with ashes and clears it away. A mother may lift her child to the edge of the bed so that it can perform on the floor, but if it is very small she often won't bother. If a baby pisses on to one's sari, nothing is done. 'He's showing how much he loves you,' I was often told. I decided I'd rather not know.

But compared to me, people were far more scrupulous about bodily cleanliness. Everyone always bathes and washes their clothes at least once a day, whatever the weather. In the winter, when it was chilly even by British standards, I occasionally gave the pleasures of complete immersion in the pond a miss, until I realised how much everyone disapproved. If I appeared in the same sari two days running I was inevitably met with cries of 'Yssh! Didn't you bathe yesterday?'

Touching rules are also different. This was something I had never really considered before: one touches certain categories of people in certain ways and places, and there's an end to it. I probably would not touch my mother on her breast, for example, but would think nothing of touching a man friend on his arm or knee in a friendly way if I knew him well. Once again, in Talukpur everything was reversed. I had to force myself not to move slightly when women I had only just met touched my face and hair, put their arms around me, or held my hand. With women who are close, lying together and caressing each other affectionately is completely normal, as are holding hands and hugging for young men who are friends. As I got to know the women better, they began to do things which I would not dream of doing at home. Having a good look at my stomach and inspecting my bra was one thing; laying both hands on my buttocks to test their relative hardness or softness was quite another!

Meanwhile, all physical contact with men was quite out of the question. At first I had to watch myself vigilantly to stop those involuntary gestures which mean nothing in Britain, but so much in Bangladesh. Married couples are equally restrained. They never touch in public, or if they do, it is only the merest brushing of hand against hand, and then only within the confines of their closest family. After about six months of this I began to worry that on my return home I would have to relearn everything all over again, or would end up shocking all my friends when I gave the women a playful squeeze in their nether regions or slapped the men in the face in outrage when they gave me a hug hello.

In that first month there were battles to be fought, too. I was regarded as totally fragile, and incapable of doing a thing for myself. I was, after all, from the mystical land of London, where everyone is fantastically rich, driven everywhere, and has never done a stroke of physical work. This view of the West is very deeply ingrained, but I fought hard to change it. Sometimes the situation verged upon the ludicrous. One of my main problems was that I could not get enough exercise in Talukpur. I told people many times that at home I loved to walk, and it was the custom of some people, including myself, to dress up in special clothes and run around until they were quite exhausted because they believed it to be good for them. But still, when I strolled across a field to visit a family they would ask if my feet hurt when I arrived, adding to each other, 'She's not used to walking, look how she suffers.'

Other people outside the village, especially those from the towns, looked stunned when I told them that I was staying in a village. The rigours of rural life were assumed to be impossible for Western softies, even though, despite the odd inconvenience, there was nothing so very hard about my life in Talukpur. Sometimes their mouths fell open when I replied that yes, I could and did eat village food, and with my fingers too, just like everyone else. The richer and more educated they were, the greater their shock. In my first weeks, my family seemed to share these assumptions. At first I was not allowed to sit anywhere but on a chair specially produced for me, help the women with their work, or do anything for myself. Full scale war broke out over who should wash my clothes. Quite reasonably, I thought, I took a pile of dirty things down to the ghat to wash them.

'Mother! What are you doing? No, no ... You must give them to us! You don't know how to! You can't!'

The clothes were snatched from me. I snatched them back. I was never going to let the women I lived with behave as if they were my servants. 'Aren't I a woman?' I asked. 'Aren't I equal? Why shouldn't I wash my own clothes?'

Pause. Then: 'Your skin is too thin, you'll hurt yourself.'

This was too much, and I stomped off to the ghat regardless. My work came in for much criticism, for of course I had washed them all wrong, and it was several months before I could wash my clothes without causing a minor scandal.

Similar fights occurred over who was to sweep and clean my room, and where I ate my food. I hated being served and insisted on eating in the kitchen, squatting on a stool by the fire and pots of rice, which I was eventually allowed to do, but only after many long and tiring arguments. The problem was that for my pride, a pretence should be made that I was just like everyone else; whereas for the family's pride, a show should be made that they had the means to treat me as a highly honoured guest.

And so I stumbled my way through those first few weeks, grappling with the language and usually not succeeding in conquering it; putting my foot in it and acting the fool: a complete and utter baby. Every night I crawled back inside my net and wondered if I would ever get used to it all, or the village people used to me. Then one day I spent the whole morning with the family women cutting up vegetables and shredding bamboo into strips with which to make baskets. Nobody commented, or seemed to think that my work was too awful. I had at last got used to squatting on my heels, and that morning I had been able to put on my sari unaided. It was then that I began to feel that, Allah willing, I might successfully learn the ropes.

2 THE LIVES THAT ALLAH GIVES

I had not been in Talukpur for long when Saleya, the eldest of my new sisters, gave birth to her fifth child. It was October, a grey day which spat rain after almost a week of continual pouring. Much of the village had been flooded and now, as far as the eye could see from the edge of the bari, there was nothing but water, with the occasional scattered patch of swamped green paddy through which the village boats glided with ease.

We were squatting in the yard stripping jute when Saleya's first labour pains began. I had already been shown how to pull the long fibres from the jute sticks and lay them out in a soggy pile on the muddy yard ground, albeit with much laughter and mock horror: 'Love! You can't do that! Yah Allah! What a smell it'll make on your hands! You're not used to it ...'

'Can't I learn? I'm not that stupid, really.'

'Katy, you will go back to your father's country and say we made you do bad things.'

'Go on, show her. This beti's quite mad.'

The other women worked quickly and skilfully, not caring when the mud splashed over their bare feet and saris. A group of poorer female relatives had come to help, in exchange for the jute sticks which they would later dry and use as firewood. They listened quietly as I was teased and admonished by the women of the household. Later they were to become important friends, but now I could hardly remember all their names, let alone who was related to whom, and how.

Saleya had been expecting her child for days, and her belly was so swollen that she had great difficulty balancing on the low wooden stools the women used. She was proud at the way she had carried on working

18

– some of her sisters and cousins had spent most of the last weeks of their pregnancies lying in the shade on mats, or tucked away behind mosquito nets complaining. But even though she had returned to her father's bari especially to give birth, she had not flagged, or used her condition as an excuse to stop work. She was a sturdy young woman of twenty-five, with hard muscular legs and arms and teeth stained red with betel. Her husband had spent many years of their marriage working in the Middle East, but he had had a holiday recently and this baby was the result.

She said nothing, but sighed 'Ya Allah' and went inside to the hard wooden bed which the women and young children used.

Amma saw her and, putting aside the soggy pile of jute she was working on, rose to follow her. 'Do you feel pain?' she asked.

Saleya nodded.

'It is the will of Allah, Daughter. Come on, we must go to the other room.'

For all births in the family, a separate room at the back of the main one was used, for birth is seen as extremely private, an affair of women, and cannot be mixed with the men's world or space; it must be kept apart, not seen and ideally not heard. Within minutes the other women in the yard had joined them, realising quickly that the time for Saleya's child had come. Only Najma and I were left, and she soon got up and went inside, saying mysteriously that she had work to do. No reference was made to her sister's condition.

I felt stupidly miserable, totally excluded in this serious business of birth, and aware of my utter uselessness. Once again I was more naive than a child. Unlike everyone else, I had not been brought up in an environment where childbirth is just a normal part of life, and I had never even seen a newborn baby.

Meanwhile, inside, Bebi and Sufia were putting mats down on the dirt floor for Saleya to lie on and some sacking to support her. They worked quickly and quietly. No one spoke of what was happening, for it would have been embarrassing and shameless openly to acknowledge her state. The wooden shutters on the windows were closed, and on hearing that the woman's 'illness' had begun, the family men made themselves scarce.

Word that 'your niece, the mother of little Hepi, her time has come' quickly reached Saleya's aunt, Kudi Bibi, in the bari next door. On hearing it she covered her head with her sari, grabbed her umbrella, and set off without further ado across the fields to join the others. She had helped at the births of all the lineage's younger children, and there had been so many of these that by now she had run out of fingers on which to count them. Perhaps she had delivered thirty, perhaps forty, she told me vaguely when I asked her, adding somewhat wearily that she could not see much point in counting such things, and Allah only knew why it should interest me.

Such work was done by only a few women in the village – the older, wiser ones who had seen many births, and almost as many deaths, and had learnt long ago from their own senior kinswomen how to open up a woman and deliver her child, what herbs to use if there were problems, and how to cut the child's cord and smear cleansing ashes on the wound. Only the week before, Kudi Bibi had been in the bari of another young wife of their lineage. It had been a terrible labour, the girl screaming and crying in fear and begging them to bring the mullah to say prayers for her, for she was sure she was going to die. It had certainly not been properly modest behaviour. The girl was saved, but her baby was born dead. They had held her all night, and tried everything to encourage the birth canals to unlock, even opening their own saris and untying their hair, but it was no good. As dawn spread itself quietly across the cool dark sky, the family decided to take the girl to Sylhet, which meant a three-hour boat journey and then the expense of a taxi to carry them over the thirty miles or so of potholed road to the hospital, but they were saved the trouble by the arrival of a baby which lay glistening and breathless on the sacking at their feet.

The old woman had seen many dead children – too many. She hardly ever spoke of her own which had not survived, but she had not forgotten them. She carried the memory of her short-lived marriage, too, wound up tightly inside her like the jute ropes the men made. After six years she had still not provided her husband with living offspring and one day, as she had been dreading, she was told that another wife was to be fetched. Her husband was a kind man and had been fond of his first bride, but he badly wanted sons and it was becoming obvious that she was not to be blessed with them. She knew that although she would still be welcome in her parents-in-law's bari, there was no real place for her now, so she had come back to her father's village and now lived in her brothers' bari. When the youngest had died, closely followed by his widow, they had left one small baby, and Kudi Bibi had not hesitated to take the child as her own. Now, Sufia was a treasured companion to her. She had taught her everything she knew, and was proud of the young woman's intelligence and abilities in the kitchen.

It did not take Kudi Bibi long to reach her niece's homestead and she went straight to the back room, telling the younger girls to heat some more water and bring her some pan to chew.

News spread quickly. By the time the midday azan had begun, Daktar, the village medicine man, had also arrived. He came clutching his wooden bag of homeopathic medicines, each labelled and carefully stored in a small glass tube, and sat outside the building on the verandah smoking *bedis* and singing loudly. He had been present when Saleya herself was born – not that he would have had anything to do with the birth, for since he was a man this would be quite impossible; rather, he came to all births to prescribe his potions and collect his fee of several *taka*. He was a member of a large Hindu bari in a nearby village, with its own special temple for Vishnu to which Muslim neighbours disparagingly referred as 'full of dolls'. On many nights the sound of drums and cries from the Hindus' worship competed with the wail of the azan.

Mobed, the eldest of Saleya's little brothers, who had already come home from his morning's lessons, was sent to the bazaar to fetch another midwife. He went off with a bag over his shoulders so that he could do the shopping at the same time, singing the love songs he had heard the week before from a theatre troupe in the market and quite oblivious to the sufferings of his sister. Kudi Bibi was experienced and knowledgeable, but the woman Mobed had been sent to fetch had a reputation for great skill. She would probably have to be given a sari for her services, for she was poor and could not work without payment, but the family were comfortable, with enough fields to keep the stores stocked with grain all year, and it was decided that the more help was available, the better. The other women gathered in the small darkened room did not even look up when she eventually arrived. Although they needed her now, she was of far lower status.

'So you've come,' Amma said. 'It is the will of Allah.'

She pulled her sari over her head and left the room to pray.

The labour was not easy, and Saleya's screams could be heard even out in the yard. Najma and Bebi did not go into her room, for as unmarried girls their presence would not have been appropriate, but sat on the steps outside looking up at the sky, or cut up betel nut to pass on a brass tray with a pile of shiny green pan leaves to the women inside. Saleya's eldest daughter, Hepi, went off alone to the ghat, and stared solemnly down at her dress whilst great tears rolled off her cheeks and plopped down on to the material. I too had retreated there, fearing that I would be in the way anywhere else. From time to time Amma appeared and came down to the water to wet her head, for with the worry it had become as hot as fire, and unless it were cooled she would not be able to carry on.

'Oh, Little Daughter!' she cried, when she saw me. 'Allah has not given me the strength for this kind of work, I can't bear it.'

'Perhaps you should get her to Sylhet, to the hospital?' I asked tentatively.

'Yah Allah, don't you know how long it takes? And how many taka! No, it is in the hands of God.'

One by one, as the sun began its descent towards the river, other family women appeared. They came bearing glasses of holy water, blessed and blown upon by the *mullah* or a boy studying at the madrasa, and covered with banana leaves; they muttered that Allah's will would be done, and prostrated themselves on the family prayer mat, murmuring the sacred Arabic words as Saleya groaned from the adjoining room. Some, who had the knowledge and skills of childbirth, joined Kudi Bibi and the other midwife, but came out looking grim and shaking their heads. Eventually Daktar drifted away, bored by the waiting and hungry for his rice, which he could never take from the family, since they were Muslim and he a Hindu, and of high caste to boot.

The sky, which was now clear of clouds, had turned from lilac to violet, and the crickets and frogs had long ago begun their evening roar, when Saleya's son was eventually born. She lay on the sacks with her bloodied sari around her and her hair falling down her back in loose wet tresses. The child, a small damp bundle, was placed by Kudi Bibi beside the livid afterbirth on a sheet of plastic matting. Kudi Bibi gave

Saleya a razor and, swaying slightly with the effort, she leant over and cut the umbilical cord. They brought lamps, which transformed the room into womb-like cosiness, and hot water to wash the child. From a special hiding place a small bottle from Mecca, the heart of Islam, was produced and very gently the baby was fed a spoonful. I was called, and stood watching them as they took turns in holding him, muttering quiet words as they supported his tiny head.

'The mother of Hepi has had a son,' they said to each other. 'Look how beautiful he is! Look at his lovely fair skin!'

I wanted more than anything to be one of them and know exactly how to hold the child and what to do, instead of an ignorant outsider.

'Give it to Katy,' Amma said, and the baby, in all its sogginess, was handed to me.

'You must name him,' Najma put in.

'Name him? No, I couldn't possibly!'

But they insisted, so I came up with an English name, which everyone smiled at politely and then immediately forgot.

Kudi Bibi brought a clay pot full of smouldering coals, and began to daub the ashes from this on the child's head and belly button to harden the skin. Then they told Saleya that it was time for her to wash. Abdul Wahid, the bari labourer, who had muscles like iron and ate an enormous amount of rice and raw chillis at every meal, had already dug a pit for this, laughing as he tossed the soft earth away with his spade. His own wife would be having another baby soon, he suspected from the way her belly was protruding, but he was a poor man and she would give birth with only the help of her mother, lying on rags in their little hut. He hoped it would be a boy. He could afford to feed another mouth only if its owner was eventually going to contribute to the rice pot.

Saleya was supported outside by Kudi Bibi and Amma, and water was poured over her while she disposed of her soiled sari and wiped the blood away from her thighs. A woman who has given birth is seen as dangerously polluted in rural Bangladesh. If her dirt or blood contaminates the place where the family wash or clean their food, great sickness is thought to ensue. More than that, it is a terrible sin. Outsiders who are wearing amulets to ward off evil spirits or help cure sickness will not go into the same room as a woman who has given birth, such is the power of her pollution (her close kin are exempt from this, for since in most households babies are born regularly, life would be impossible were they not). In theory the rules continue for forty days, although in practice a woman's confinement is often shorter. The new mother should not leave the household during this time, for her impurities make her vulnerable to the 'bad airs' and evil spirits which lurk outside. Whilst presented in terms of the dangers facing mother and child, the taboos also mean both can rest and bond with each other before engaging with the world beyond their household. She should also eat only 'soft' foods. This means no curries or any of the strength-giving ingredients they contain – no meat, fish or eggs: all are forbidden. For at least a fortnight, Saleya could expect only bread and ghee or rice with powdered milk and biscuits. That the family could afford to follow these traditional restrictions, and had such choice in their foodstuffs, even if they did have to budget carefully to afford the special ingredients for Saleya, was a sign of their relative prosperity.

After her bath, Saleya was left alone while the women fussed and clucked over the child. They sent for the mullah for amulets and tied them around the baby's pink, wizened body to protect it from the ghosts and spirits which might steal its soul and kill it. Then Kudi Bibi painted a large black spot on to its forehead to shield it from the evil eye. A tiny baby's life is an uncertain thing, and too many are lost for such precautions not to be taken. Villagers can do little if a child does become ill, and the age-old charms at least give them some feeling of control.

When Abba returned at last from the bazaar and heard that he had a new grandson, he nodded in pleasure and, placing his prayer cap firmly on to his head, went to the edge of the birth room and sang out loud Arabic prayers. Later, back in Saleya's husband's village, an *akika* (birth celebration) would be held for the new member of the family. The lineage elders would come, a cow would be sacrificed and prayers would be said as the child was formally named. After his prayer the old man shuffled off to his hookah and many of the women drifted back to their work. Guests dropped by and grunted in approval when they heard of the birth, then returned to their talk of fields and village politics and family news. Childbirth is nothing special, for it happens all the time; nearly every household has at least one young baby and as this grows older, it is soon replaced by another.

The next day, this time without Saleya, we were once more in the yard with piles of muddy jute in front of us. Banessa, a poor woman from outside the village who would be given a small basketful of rice in return for her work, was telling of how in her village the wife of one of the most important men had had an 'operation'. Banessa was known for her loudness and vulgarity, and often broke into crude songs which she sang at the top of her voice and which the bari women pretended to be horrified by, but secretly enjoyed. Pausing from her work, she wiped her mucky hands over her tatty sari as she spoke. The difference between her and the others was radical. She was almost as thin and brittle as the sticks of jute, and wore her faded sari without blouse or petticoat. Her toughened legs were covered only to the shins, and she displayed the silver-coloured bangles of widowhood on her tiny wrists.

'She's had it done,' she was saying. 'Her husband took her into Sylhet and now she's all closed up.'

The others muttered in astonishment, not sure whether it was a good or a sinful thing to do. They had also heard tales of doctors coming to villages and giving injections to stop the babies, but that had never happened in Talukpur.

'She has children?' asked Amma.

'Four: three boys and one girl.'

'Then that is good.'

The others nodded. Four was certainly a good number, as long as there were sons amongst them. But most women could expect at least seven or eight children, if not more. What could they do? Their husbands wanted them, and Allah sent them.

'Too many babies destroy a woman's body,' someone else said. She had endured ten pregnancies, and now had seven surviving children. She had been renowned for her blooming beauty when she was a bride, with a plump face and arms and the gentle freshness of a sixteen-year-old. Now her face was drawn and her body thin and shrivelled. I smiled at her supportively. Contraception was something I was not so ignorant about. I even had a book about teaching grass-roots health care in rural communities, with pictures of all the different ways and means of preventing the babies, and fascinating diagrams of women in labour. Over the coming year the fame of this book was to spread widely, and I was frequently asked to show it to women who came to my room and inquired in hushed whispers whether I still had 'that doctor's book' which they had heard of.

'But how is it done, this operation?'

Nobody knew.

Banessa chuckled, and then with a mischievous grin turned to one of the younger women who had been married only a couple of months and still, as a new bride, kept her sari drawn over her head and her mouth shut.

'Eh, Elder Sister, you should get your husband to buy those balloons from the bazaar before you're destroyed by children like us ... '

Everyone knew what she was talking about – the pink condoms which the children blew up as balloons and played with for days. But the new bride did not wait to hear more: overcome with embarrassment and shame, she covered her face with her sari and went running inside.

'Chup!' the women cried at Banessa. 'Ma, look how this woman talks; she has no shame at all!'

But Banessa, still laughing to herself about the pink balloons which were so successful with the children, had broken into song: 'Oh, Lover, why have you left me?' she sang in her rough, rasping voice.

'What wrong have I done?
Is it not so that Krishna has many wives?
Is it not so that he watches them bathe in the great river?
When you come back you will bring new saris.
I will cover my bed with red flowers.
I will feed you sweets as we sit upon its covers ...

Here, she broke into a long raucous chuckle and clapped her hands in glee.

The other women tutted mildly and then began again to shred the damp jute, working quickly and efficiently until the pile of stalks was almost finished.

3 HUSHNIA GETS MARRIED

Suddenly and miraculously, just when I had decided that my whole body was destined to rot away in the damp, the weather changed. The skies cleared, and the days became bright; dawns were pink with the rising sun and grey with mist, and the former midday heat became merely a pleasant warmth. The evenings were filled with golden light and birdsong. It grew cold, too; we all had heavy covers on our beds at night, and I was pleased that I had packed a pair of socks.

The country was transformed. Where there had previously been water, within a week fields appeared. I discovered that I could now walk from bari to bari, and did not have to find someone to take me by boat. My world was slowly expanding. Even the river which ran through the village eventually turned into paddy land.

As soon as the paths had dried out and the rice, which had been a startlingly bright green when I arrived, turned yellow, the village came to life. There were always people now on the tracks leading between villages – clusters of women in burquas going visiting with their children, the occasional rickshaw jolting along, young men on bicycles, village swells on motorbikes, and old gents in their best white *punjabis* strolling to the bazaar.

By late November, the harvest had begun. All month people from the poorer parts of the country had been arriving for the work, coming by launch and bus and foot, with bundles of belongings on their heads and babies tucked under their arms. The village swelled. Straw huts sprang up for the migrants, and at night one could see their fires and hear their songs and the screams of their children all down the river banks.

Every morning at dawn, the workers would leave for the fields. They were a merry crowd who sang incessantly at the tops of their voices

27

when they were out cutting the paddy. During the day the household children carried great vats of rice out to them, and by late afternoon they would return, carrying huge bundles of the crop hanging from poles balanced on their shoulders. Long past sunset the bari yard was full of activity. Abba took his chair out into the open and smoked his hookah with satisfaction as he watched his harvest being threshed. The men often stayed awake most of the night, singing and reciting stories.

Now that the fields had appeared, and people could move from village to village without sinking into six feet of mud, the wedding season started. There had already been some marriages during the monsoon, the groom's party moving by brightly decorated boats that blared out Hindi film songs and exploded with the sounds of firecrackers, much to my initial alarm; but this was nothing like the quantity of weddings which took place during the winter when, after the confines of heat and rain, the villages seemed almost to burst with reawakened life and vigour.

Hushnia, the daughter of Abba's cousin, was married in January. The rice had now been processed, and in the cool nights and warm days the villagers could relax a little and enjoy the most pleasant season of the year. There had been talk of the forthcoming wedding for weeks.

'Is it true she's to be married?' women visiting our bari asked.

'Is it true that he's a mullah? The son of Abu Meer's mother's brother?'

'It's right that she should be given in marriage now,' others commented. 'She's already at least twenty, and wasn't her elder sister taken by her husband when she was sixteen?'

It was true, she had been of marriageable age for some years now, staying on her father's bari long after her education had finished. She was a pretty girl, too, with long black hair which came down to her bottom, and bright eyes. Everyone knew, although they did not mention it, that her father had experienced difficulties in raising enough money to pay for her dowry. In Talukpur this meant the provision of household goods for the new couple by the bride's family. Two fields had been sold to someone from outside the village, and her mother, a fat and usually docile woman, was wont to complain loudly at her fate in having six daughters and only one son.

In her own bari, which lay next to ours, Hushnia was teased mercilessly. Her younger cousins and sisters, who did not yet have to worry about what would eventually – and inevitably – happen to them, took a malicious delight in their whisperings, which made her pale with fear and leave the room.

'Your husband is going to be a mullah, with a great bushy beard!' they'd cry, and then explode into giggles and run away.

The rumours were not without foundation. Although except for these frightening hints Hushnia knew nothing of it, negotiations over the marriage had already been taking place for several weeks. Both her family and that of the prospective husband had been communicating through Abdul Chalan, the son of a village neighbour, and all concerned were pleased with the relative status and prosperity of their in-laws-to-be. All that remained was for a party of representatives from the groom's family to 'view' her, making sure that she did not have any major defects and was as beautiful and modest as the young middleman had assured them.

'Are you going over to our *sassa's* [father's brother's] bari today?' Najma asked me one morning. She was standing by the chest in the women's room, combing oil into her hair. The new silky shalwar kameez and orna she was wearing were testimony to the fact that she was going visiting.

'Why?'

'The people from Hushnia's groom's bari are coming. Amma and sassi [father's brother's wife] have already gone. There'll be lots of *misti.*'

I never turned down the chance of misti (sweetmeat) handouts, my sweet tooth having finally got the better of me in Bangladesh, and gladly walked with Najma across the fields to her cousin's bari. I wanted to talk to her about her own marriage, which had been gossiped about for months now, but dared not raise the subject, since the last time I had tried she had disappeared furiously inside, her silence and swift departure a sign that she had no intention of discussing such sensitive and embarrassing things with me. I was, after all, in the position of her elder sister, with whom such talk was strictly taboo. I hated the fact that I knew far more about the arrangements which were being made for her life than she did herself, but had learnt my lesson. My aborted attempt had caused her to stonily avoid me for days.

By the time we arrived at sassi's bari, Hushnia had been long installed in her bed, hiding under a counterpane as her unmarried female kin sat around her and giggled. The women of the lineage had been cooking frantically all morning. There was sweetened milk to be prepared – an absolute must when entertaining potential in-laws – puddings and sweetmeats, and then the extravagance of a chicken curry; several pools of splattered blood in the yard indicated that more than one chicken had been killed, so important were these guests. A table had been set out specially in one of the rooms, with all the best crockery, dusty and unused from the youngest uncle's wife's dowry, and a plastic tablecloth. Hushnia's old grandfather had changed into his best punjabi and starched prayer cap for their reception, and was sitting expectantly in the yard waiting for the party to appear. Najma sped quickly past him, covering her head with her orna as a mark of respect. Hushnia's father had recently gone to Saudi to find work, and by the time he was to return his daughter would already have been married for several years.

At last they arrived. There were five of them: four young men in their best trousers and shirts, and a little girl aged about twelve in a frilly dress and high-heeled sandals which were too big for her, but which her elder sister had lent specially for the occasion. They were seated in the guest room, while the bari men slowly appeared and sat opposite them, asking polite questions. When Hushnia's grandfather was eventually seated in the centre of the room the conversation turned to religious matters, and the greatness of Allah, which effectively unblocked the conversation, for it was something which all the men had much to say about, and they were anxious to show each other just how pious their respective families were. The women peered through the slats in the bamboo partition which divided the rooms.

'What are they like?' they whispered to each other.

'Are they black?'

'Katy, go and talk to them and tell us what they say to you.'

'No, I can't, it wouldn't be right.'

More to the point, in such a highly formal situation, it would be a dead bore, and I hated being shown off as the village freak. Anyway, I had my modesty to think of, a sure excuse.

'I'd be ashamed,' I added.

After the feast, during which the conversation had turned to the madrasa education of one of the boys in the family and the fact that Hushnia's grandfather had performed *Haj*, the pilgrimage to Mecca, it was time to view the would-be bride. In the next room, where she shared a large bed with her three younger sisters, Hushnia had covered her face with her sari and turned her back to the people sitting around her. She was sobbing quietly to herself when her elder brother came and leant over her.

'Take this to the guests, Sister,' he told her, handing her a brass tray of pan leaves, betel, and pots of spices and lime. She slowly turned over and hauled herself out of bed. She never dared to refuse her elder brother. Hiding as much of her face as possible with her sari, she walked hesitantly into the guests' room and, keeping her eyes fixed on the floor, offered the pan tray to one of the young men.

'What's your name?' he asked.

She muttered that it was Hushnia Begum.

'What class?' another inquired.

'Five.'

'She can read and write,' her brother put in. 'She writes letters for her mother to her father in Saudi. Write your address, Sister.'

They brought her a pen and one of the children's school books, and with a trembling hand she wrote her name, and those of the village and the local bazaar, in as clear and beautiful a hand as she could muster. The guests seemed satisfied.

'You can go now,' her elder brother told her, and she fled.

Later on, a small party from Hushnia's family would make the journey to the groom's village to meet him and continue the marriage negotiations. They were rigorously cross-questioned − although not by Hushnia, who was very much absent − when they returned. What was the groom like? Was he beautiful? Did he really have a beard? What had they been given to eat? Was his skin fair or dark? Had they *salaamed* them? (a customary gift of money as a token gesture in marriage negotiations).

The answers were all pleasing, and it was decided that the marriage should go ahead. There were many more meetings between Abdul Chalan and the two families after this stage had been reached. Each party had to discuss how much they would give the other. The groom's family should provide saris, a burqua, shoes, make-up, and the all-important gold jewellery for the bride, in addition to gifts of clothing for her immediate family, whilst Hushnia's kin should hold the wedding feast and give all the articles necessary to set the new couple up – a bed, chairs, a wardrobe and table, glasses, crockery, and so on. If they had been really rich they would have given a television (and a car battery to power it) or perhaps a motorbike, but they could not stretch to this.

Nobody spoke to Hushnia about her forthcoming marriage, and she asked no questions. Like Najma, she knew that to remain modest, she must keep quiet. The only woman she could have approached might have been her *babi* (elder brother's wife), with whom she enjoyed a very open relationship, but they were rarely alone. She was far too ashamed and shy ever to raise the subject with her elder sisters, and with her mother or brother it was quite out of the question. But the teasing continued, and she gathered that her husband was going to be 'as black as the night', and his family was very orthodox. 'He's a mullah!' her cousins told her, meaning that he had studied at a madrasa; but she looked away and refused to lower her dignity by replying.

Hushnia's was not the only marriage being arranged in Talukpur that month. In a mud and bamboo hut across the river, wedding plans were also being made, but in far greater secrecy. On the afternoon that Hushnia handed the betel tray round, Wahed Ullah squatted in his dirt yard picking his teeth and scowling. His wife was howling inside while neighbours peered through the trees surrounding the bari to see what was happening. He shouted at a group of children to get off his land, and spat on the ground.

He had announced that he intended to bring another wife to the bari. The old one had borne him six children, and now she had grown haggard and ugly. He had friends in the bazaar and they had told him of a girl who was available. She was poor, and not of good family. Even worse, she had been married before, but her husband had taken off after a year. Someone had whispered that there had been a baby – dead now, but still, that had lowered her value even more. Her family, then, were glad of this chance of getting another husband for her. If she was to be a second wife, well, it couldn't be helped.

So it was all fixed. There would be no feast or exchange of gifts. In a week's time her uncle would bring her to Wahed Ullah's bari, and that would be that. Why should he tell anyone of his plans? He was the head of the family and it was his right to take a second wife if he so chose. Other men did, and other men's wives accepted it, so why did his have to make such a fuss? She had screamed that they could hardly feed all their children, let alone another woman and the babies that would no doubt follow. Why had he done this just when he'd sold the last of their land? Didn't he have to support his old widowed mother and divorced sister too?

He hated the sound of her complaints. No woman should ever question her husband's actions. This was his order, and she could accept the new wife or get out. But she had followed him into the yard, and when she yelled that she'd never agree to his plans he had hit her hard across the face. She had fallen down, and now she was wailing that her arm was broken. He'd had enough. Well, if it was broken, it was for the best; then he would have to get a second wife as this one wouldn't be able to do any work. He spat again and shouted at his daughter to bring him his afternoon meal.

Two weeks later the first part of Hushnia's marriage took place. Elders from her lineage, the groom's lineage, and the village Imam came to her, and she formally said *'Kabul'* in agreement. After this, the menfolk went to the district town to register the union officially. This was men's business, and did not include Hushnia. It was arranged that the second part of the marriage, when Hushnia would be taken to her husband's bari, would follow ten days later. Since her family were old-fashioned, the couple would not meet until then. Some families in the village allowed their daughters to meet and even sleep with their husbands after the first stage of marriage, but Hushnia's grandfather had strongly vetoed this idea.

There was no avoiding what was to happen to her now. Bits of furniture for her dowry began to appear from the bazaar, looking ungainly and overly new as they blocked up the verandah. Relatives started to arrive – Hushnia's aunt and her daughters from Sylhet, a cousin and her husband from a nearby village. Her brother set out one morning in his best lungi, with his umbrella arched against the sun and a pile of envelopes tucked under his arm. Hushnia saw him leave as she squatted down by the ghat doing the family washing, and knew that they were invitations to her wedding for the other village families. She stopped singing, as she usually did when she worked, and began to avoid everyone's company.

'Hushnia's sulking!' her cousins laughed.

The days of her freedom from in-laws and marital responsibility sped quickly past. She knew that she would never again belong on her father's bari which, except for the odd visit to relatives in Sylhet, she had never left before. She was to be married on Friday.

Thursday night loomed, and she sat numb and silent as the family women bustled around her. The bari was overflowing now with relatives. It was a scene of barely controlled chaos. Women sat hunched over their *das* (long blades placed on the floor) cutting onions, potatoes, garlic. Hushnia's brother counted the wedding gifts and made a long inventory of what had been given and all the things which would go to her inlaws' bari; children ran around screaming with excitement and letting off firecrackers. Most of the village elders had assembled in the *bangla-ghor* (separate room for male guests) to give their formal approval of the forthcoming union. All weddings in the village took place only with the agreement of the lineage heads.

Later that night, the girls hauled an old cassette-recorder from the cabinet where precious things were kept, and with much laughter started to play tapes of Hindi film music, the love songs which they never dared sing when the elders were around. When Hushnia's babi arrived, wiping her hands on her sari after hours of work in the kitchen, they began to paint her hands with *henna*, working slowly and painstakingly over the intricate designs.

'Oh, the new son-in-law is waiting for us in the guest room,' Hushnia's babi began to sing quietly. 'We must bring him bananas, we must bring him sweets.'

All the women knew the old wedding songs by heart, and loved a chance to sing them in their low, chanting voices.

'Come, help me fill my water pot, Love, down by the banian tree,' sang someone else and the others joined in, clapping their hands, 'make waves in the water until it is filled with gold.'

Then the song disintegrated into laughter, and they started a new one. By the time they had finished, and the henna on Hushnia's hands had stained her skin a deep red, it was 3 a.m. and the bari was filled with the sounds of snoring. One by one the young women fell asleep, their arms flung out around each other, until only Hushnia was left awake, staring at the white spirals of moonlight falling down on to her bed.

Tomorrow it would all be different. She was to be married and taken to another village, far away from home. She could no longer sit laughing with her cousins, or play pranks with her little brothers. It would be many months before she would even return for more than a few nights. All the small freedoms which she had taken for granted were ending. From now on she must be respectable and modest, a grown woman. She knew exactly what was expected of her, for she had seen many brides, all of them silent, with downcast eyes, as people had crowded around to get a look at them. And like all the village girls, she had heard many stories of wicked mothers-in-law, beatings, and wives complaining that they were not fed enough. She had learnt too of babies, handsome husbands and wedding gold, but tonight such joys seemed distant indeed. Even the words which Hushnia's cousins had been singing earlier on spoke only of the tragedy of marriage:

'Tomorrow I am going to a new country, where my relatives cannot come; They will carry me off on my death casket, and I will wear a shroud for my groom ...

She dabbed her eyes with her sari. It was terrifying.

Then suddenly the azan began, and Hushnia saw that the sky was brightening. The dawn had crept up behind her and caught her unawares. Her grandfather was already muttering his prayers and the servant girl had started banging pots around in the kitchen. It was Friday already, the day she was going to be married.

We set out early that morning to Sassa's bari. Several hours had been spent in elaborate preparation. Best silk saris were carefully folded into place, hair was oiled, flowers were fixed to the backs of buns and plaits, and yellow *holud* (root plant) juices smeared into skin to make it fairer. As usual, I was not as smart as the family would have wished. My sari never came down far enough to cover my feet, I had no pretty sandals with delicate heels, just decaying plastic flip-flops, and I resolutely allowed my sari to slip away from my head.

Amma had already gone to the 'wedding bari' the day before, and spent the night there. Abba would be coming later, joining the groom's party at the mosque for the communal Friday prayer. He always looked most impressive dressed up for best. In his white punjabi and lungi, with his fine Calcutta walking stick over his arm, he was a picture of village respectability. As he strode off towards the village tea-stalls, today was no exception.

'So you're going to the marriage of Hushnia, are you, Beti?' he'd asked me earlier, his eyes twinkling with some secret joke. 'Are you going to fill your belly with our wedding food?'

By the time Najma, Hepi and I arrived, the bari had already been a site of frenzied activity for many hours. Young men had begun to build a bamboo archway at the entrance to the compound with a big sign hanging over it, reading 'Welcome' in Bengali, English and Arabic. Chairs and tables were set up under a canopy for the wedding feast, and big vats of beef curry were already being carried outside. The pile of presents had seemingly doubled and the inventory was rechecked, added to, and checked again. There was a brief panic when it was realised that the punjabi shirt promised to Hushnia's new father-in-law had been forgotten, but this was remedied by a speedy trip to the bazaar. In the kitchen, huge pots of rice and biriani were prepared by the women, and piles of plates and glasses were gathered and cleaned for the guests.

Many of them had already arrived. The women came in selfconsciously in their best saris and wedding gold, clutching their children and trying not to get their saris crumpled. Everyone was very polite at first. But soon the crush intensified, and as the business of cooking took over from formalities, most of the women forgot about spoiling their clothing and ended up squatting on the floor, cutting betel nut and vegetables and gossiping. Outside, village elders who had come early were settled on chairs in the yard and sat perusing the scene. Old Saiyed Ali, an elder from one of the most influential families in the village, had been given the best place under the shade of a large mango tree. He, more than anyone, was always shown the utmost respect. Hushnia's brother fetched his father's hookah for him and dutifully answered his questions: Yes, the in-laws were a good family, the groom was class ten; yes, a very generous settlement; oh yes, he has extremely fair skin, too.

At noon Hushnia was bathed by her babi. She felt terrible. She had not been able to eat anything that morning, despite her mother's attempts to fill her up with rice, and her head throbbed. Her babi led her to the water pump, whilst the other women and children watched, and spread holud on her face and arms as she sat submissively beneath the efficient hands.

'Oh, she will be so beautiful!' the women said. 'Don't forget her feet, Sheema – Yah Allah! Those firecrackers!'

Then they scattered seeds of rice and grasses on her hair to symbolically ensure her fertility and happiness, and helped her into a dry sari. From now onwards she would not move without the help of their hands. With the guiding gestures of her family women, who pulled the material around her, smoothed her hair, and took total control, she was turning into a meek and passive bride. Her mother hung back and watched from the kitchen doorway. She had started to cry when she saw her daughter's ritual cleansing, and she blew her nose out noisily on to the dirt floor. Her fate was not good. Six daughters, and she would lose all of them to another family.

Then the news came: they had arrived ... the groom had arrived! The women rushed to the verandah and peered through the gaps in the bamboo wall. They could see a large group of strangers entering the yard, but did not have time to glimpse the groom, for now that the party had appeared, they had to be fed. They ran to the kitchens and started to dole out huge quantities of food, while the household men hauled the vast cauldrons outside to the waiting guests. Suddenly everyone was eating. The women sat around on the beds and shared plates of *biriani*, but not until they were sure that outside, the groom's party had started to tuck into their mutton. Then there was sweetened yoghurt, rice pudding, and piles of pan and betel to get through. Everyone knew that the first question their guests would be asked when they returned home was 'What did they give you to eat?'

At last the eating was finished, and Hushnia's brother appeared with a suitcase. The women gathered round, and it was flung open. There were so many people that some of them fetched chairs to stand on, so that they could get a better view. Everything was there, as had been promised. The groom's family had not forgotten a thing – hair oil and kohl, petticoats and blouses. The women pulled the wedding gold from its paper wrapping, weighing it in their hands and nodding in approval. There were two pairs of huge earrings, and a small gold ring with a red stone. Hushnia had also been given red bangles, sandals and face powder, and a pure white burqua. At last they came to the wedding sari. It was deep red and heavy with gold embroidery, worth at least two thousand taka (about £40). They sighed as they fingered it. It was not from Sylhet, but from Dhaka. They ran critical fingers over the needlework, and said it could probably have been better quality for the price. The gold was certainly beautiful but, they decided, their families had given better saris to their brides. There was not enough time for more discussion; the feast was over now, and Hushnia had to be prepared.

So many people were squeezed into the room that movement was barely possible. Hushnia was gently helped on to the bed and her cousins and sisters gathered around her, working swiftly. They painted an intricate design on to her forehead with red nail varnish, and tied plastic flowers into her hair. Then they spread powder on her face and slipped the bangles on to her wrists.

'Do sit still, Sister!' they told her. 'You'll smudge the make-up.'

But she was not listening, for suddenly her eyelids began to flicker, and with a slight sigh she slumped down.

The crowd pressed around more closely. 'What's happened?' they cried. People could no longer get into the room. The children and young girls, who were all desperate to see, hung on to the windows outside and peeked through the cracks in the walls.

'Hushnia has fainted!'

The word spread like the waters of a flooded river. Elder women who were still in the kitchens, or sorting through the suitcase of gifts, came running. Kudi Bibi was first. She pushed her way through the crowd and shook the girl, whilst Najma, always efficient in a crisis, poured water on her face.

'Hushnia!' Kudi Bibi shouted. Her usually kind and calm face was tight with irritation. Sweat was dripping from her forehead on to her niece's wedding sari. Another aunt began to fan Hushnia furiously, but it was no good. Her brother arrived, his punjabi damp with heat, and shook her even harder.

'Hushnia!' he cried. 'Hushnia! Wake up! We're late already! Open your eyes! They're waiting to take you!'

But she did not even twitch. Her mother burst into tears, and ran out of the room. Eventually they decided that they should call the elders. One by one they came: first her uncle and grandfather, then another uncle, and eventually even Saiyed Ali. They all had different remedies. One man pinched her nose; another, who had had a madrasa education, muttered some Arabic words and blew on to her face. I privately reckoned a good strong dose of brandy would do the trick, but wisely kept my mouth shut. However jokingly made, a comment like that would hardly have enhanced my reputation.

What was to be done? It was already four o'clock, and the groom's party was becoming impatient. Inside the bari, the elders stood around and argued anxiously amongst themselves. Should they proceed as if nothing had happened, wrap her up in her burqua and hand her over anyway, or should they tell the groom that the bride he had come to collect was ill? Surely, Allah willing, she would open her eyes soon? But the minutes on the large clock with an inscription in Arabic on its face – part of her dowry ticked past, and she did not. Hushnia's family began to grow angry. This wedding was the will of Allah, and the girl should be grateful. She was damaging the honour of their lineage. She was doing this intentionally. All women must marry and leave their homes. She could not avoid it by fainting.

And the truth of the matter was that they were right: she couldn't. Whether Hushnia's swoon was deliberate or not, it would do nothing to avert something which most young girls in the village would eventually face – marriage to a strange man, and exile from her parental home. Hushnia had also not reckoned on Banessa, who was watching the scene intently as she squatted by the bamboo partition and chewed a lump of betel. She had been in the bari all day, working hard in the kitchen in return for a small basketful of rice and a dish of biriani. Away from the keen eyes of Hushnia's mother she had also managed to secrete into the folds of her sari some of the sweetmeats, which she would give to her children when she reached home. She always made a point of being around when there was a wedding; the richer families invariably needed her help, and were too busy to spend time arguing with her over how much they would pay. Banessa, like the other destitute women in the village, was used to being on the edges of another family's celebrations, watching the other women show off the gold, and the silk saris she would never possess. She was delighted just to be given an old cast-off sari.

Banessa stood up and pushed her way towards Hushnia. She had a reputation for healing skills and a knowledge of herbal medicine; and although she was known for being vulgar, and not altogether respectable, she was also known for being wise: women in the baris she worked for often went to her with their aches and pains. Now she knew exactly what to do. Attention was briefly off Hushnia, as the elders discussed what they should do, so few people noticed the skinny servant woman push herself up to the girl's bed. Banessa leant over her and, taking her hand, pinched it with knowing precision on the palm. Hushnia's eyes opened immediately with the pain, and she sat up. The moment she realised where she was she started to wail, but despite her sobs she was now quite conscious.

Banessa smiled into her eyes. 'Eh, Elder Sister,' she whispered, 'your groom is waiting for you.'

Hushnia closed her eyes, and streams of tears ran down her cheeks. There were to be no more delays now, and her cousins and sisters set to work on her again. They fixed the gold jewellery to her ears and around her neck, quickly wrapped her into the sari, and spread the red-tinselled orna of marriage over her head. Then they buttoned her into the burqua. Outside, a *shwari* (covered sedan chair for carrying brides) was waiting to bear her away.

At last the groom was brought in. He was a sallow young man with serious brown eyes and shaking hands. The women did not think him handsome — in fact he looked slightly ridiculous in his gold wedding coat and turban. They guessed that he was at least thirty. He touched the elder women's feet and took the taka they offered him. Hushnia was led to him by her brother, on whom she leant heavily, crying profusely as she took her unwilling steps towards her new husband. Both were fed sweetmeats as they sat with downcast eyes. Slowly, methodically, as she knew she should, she then knelt at the young man's feet and touched them with her hands. All her life she had heard the old saying: 'A woman's Heaven is at her husband's feet.' This man was now her husband, and these were his feet. She still had not dared to look at his face.

Then her mother came to her, and she threw herself on her neck, sobbing. 'Don't make me go, Ma! Don't make me go!' she screamed.

But her brother gathered her up in his arms and lifted her firmly to the shwari. She was bundled inside, and as two labourers swung it on to their shoulders the groom and his party walked in a procession to a waiting car on the dirt track, without more ado.

The women ran to the edge of the bari and watched through the trees screening it off as Hushnia was carried to the car, which was splendidly bedecked with tinsel. The groom and his party followed behind in a great swarm. For many minutes they could still make out his thin shoulders and gold turban. Her mother fancied that she could still hear her daughter crying.

'Yah Allah,' she sighed as she wiped her eyes with the edge of her sari. 'Ah, Hushnia, what will your life be?'

Everyone was crying – even Banessa, who had not even liked Hushnia, for the girl had always ordered her around with the utmost contempt. But she was also thinking about the three sweet pastries which she had taken from the pot in the kitchen, and the fullness of her belly. She saw me and put her arm around my back, even though I towered above her.

'Eh, Elder Sister, will you cry like that when your husband comes for you? Will you give me an invitation to come and eat rice at your wedding?'

'Of course, Banessa, but I shan't be getting married again. I already have ten husbands back in London.'

And laughing heartily at my stupid joke, which Banessa probably half-believed, we linked hands and walked out of the bari into the deep gold evening light.

As Hushnia was being taken to her new home, a man and a young woman were walking over the fields into the village. He wore his best – in fact his only – lungi, and she was covered by a heavy black burqua in the old-fashioned style, which left only a grid for her eyes. He held her by the arm as they walked, and they did not speak. The path, which had followed the river, took them through one side of Talukpur. When they reached the small cluster of huts which formed the bari of Wahed Ullah, the man turned abruptly and walked through the makeshift screen of dried banana leaves which sheltered it from public gaze. The bari women, who were sitting in the yard picking through each other's hair for lice, jumped up with shock at the stranger's appearance and ran inside for cover. The man called for Wahed Ullah and he came out, for he had been waiting for them. He shouted at his wife to bring their guest tea and rice, and did not look at the covered figure standing by the door.

Later the mullah came and the girl whispered her 'Kabul'. They had put her in a tiny room at the back of the kitchen. It had been quickly and hastily erected; its rough mud walls had large gaps in them and the banana leaves and sheets of plastic which formed the roof only partially shut out the sky. She sat on a mat on the floor in a worn sari with her face covered. If a visitor came in, she stood up and turned to the wall. When told to, she would kneel down and touch the visitor's feet. The bari women brought her food, but they did not speak to her. They did not want her there, although they knew they must accept her. Wahed Ullah's first wife would not even pull the girl's sari back from her face and look at her. She still could not sleep for the pain in her arm. Other villagers did not come to see the new wife, either. There were no gifts, and no new saris.

'She is not a wife, but a servant girl,' Amma said disdainfully. 'Why should I go to that stupid cousin's house to visit his servant?'

And so the marriage of Wahed Ullah was ignored by most people. His lineage elders were displeased, but he was not important to them, so they did not try to prevent it. After a while people stopped discussing the disreputable way in which the marriage had been arranged. Eventually, too, the new wife was accepted by the others. She worked hard, and had a pretty face, and they soon became fond of her. The unexpected unity of the women did not, however, make her husband any better tempered, and when the girl appeared several weeks later with a fresh black eye, everyone knew that she was now truly a part of things, a fully fledged member of Wahed Ullah's household.

Meanwhile, amongst Hushnia's family, it was generally agreed that the wedding had been a great success. As always, the lineage had appeared in its most honourable light. The food was good and plentiful, the guests of high social standing, the gifts to the in-laws bountiful and, as the occasion demanded, the bride had cried. For many days after she had been taken off in her shwari the women of the bari discussed it, and reminisced over every detail.

'Oh, how beautiful it was!' they declared.

'How she cried!'

'What a lovely sari she had ... '

Then they thought of their own marriages, and most of them smiled to themselves before sighing slightly and turning back to their work.

4 A WOMAN'S PLACE

On the evening of Hushnia's wedding, I went to visit Sufia in the small thatch and bamboo house she shared with Kudi Bibi. She was squatting in the kitchen, rolling out *pitas* (rice cakes) into small triangles when I arrived, and I happily joined her. It was one of the easier culinary tasks, and I had almost mastered it. From time to time Sufia would hold a pita up and declare, 'This is a woman, and this one, a man!' and then collapse helplessly with laughter. The bari was virtually empty, since everyone was still at Hushnia's homestead, and Kudi Bibi would not be back for many hours. It was a good time to ask her about marriage. With just the two of us there, she could tell me many things and would not be ashamed.

'Of course I cried at my wedding,' she said, casting a critical eye over my handiwork, taking one of the pitas I had just completed and rerolling it with a skilled hand. 'Every woman cries at her wedding. If she didn't, people would say that she was bad. They'd start whispering, and say "That girl has no shame." Did Hushnia cry a lot? Didn't you like the wedding?'

I replied that she had, that I hadn't liked it, and that in my country we were happy to get married. Shocking as it might be, we usually loved our husbands before we married them.

'Ah well, your country is different. You Londoni people have one way, and we have another.'

'But don't you feel sorry for Hushnia?'

'Katy, you don't understand.'

She was right. I didn't understand how she could be sitting there so complacently, telling me that arranged marriages were fine, crying was great, and weddings were lovely, especially as she'd been through it herself.

'Listen. Hushnia is only crying because she must leave her parents' home, where she has been all her life. She's not crying about her husband. She knows that all women must marry, and that is what Allah willed. What would happen to her life if she had no marriage? She trusts her parents that they'll find someone good for her. Don't they love her? They have found her a fine husband. Perhaps in your country people don't cry because they are always separate from their parents – that's true, isn't it? Slowly Hushnia and our new brother-in-law will start to love each other. You'll see.'

She paused, and then added softly, 'I remember the words of my husband every moment that I am awake.'

Later that week we walked across the fields to one of the lineage baris to see a new bride. She had been brought back from her father's village the evening before in a ramshackle minibus decorated with tinsel which had raised great clouds of dust as it bounced along the country track. She was to be the new wife of yet another of my family's cousins.

The bari was crammed full of people. All the rooms were overflowing with guests sitting on the beds and chairs, while inside great piles of food were endlessly served.

'Have you seen our bride?' Rahela, the groom's youngest sister, asked after touching our noses with hers, in greeting. 'She's not beautiful. Black!' And then she laughed and hurried past. Later on, I was to realise that to insult one's new babi is the order of the day, marking the beginning of an informal and jokey relationship.

The bridal chamber was even fuller than the other rooms. Toddlers screamed and pushed, and old women in starched white saris sat with their hands on their laps, looking at the scene with approval. In the middle of a mass of teenage girls and overexcited children, sitting on the bed with her face covered and her head down, was the new bride. They were fingering her hair and her bangles, tugging the veil from her head as she vainly tried to pull it back, and examining her hands. From time to time she dabbed at her eyes with her handkerchief.

'Come and see her!' they cried when they saw me. They seized her face and pushed the veil roughly back, then forced her eyelids open with their fingers. She was lovely.

'Hello,' I said lamely, 'my name's Katy. What's yours?'

But of course she didn't reply, just looked away in horror.

'Do you think she's beautiful?' a little girl decorated for the festivities with great patches of red rouge on her cheeks and lips, and plastic flowers in her hair, asked me. She thrust a sticky hand into mine. 'The new babi's so black!'

'No, don't be rude. She's very pretty. Wait till you have to be married and then you'll be less of a horrible little girl.'

The remark had its desired effect, for the hand was instantly withdrawn and the child screamed in terrified embarrassment at my risque mention of her future. Little girls learn their roles young, and know they must be ashamed at the prospect that one day they too might be married. The other children squealed in delight and continued to press around the bride, pulling at her orna and heavy gold earrings while she shook with sobs.

The young woman's ordeal was to last for three days, as it does for all new brides in a conventional marriage. After this, as is the local tradition, she was taken back to her father's bari for a visit, to cushion the jolt of marriage and exile. Like Hushnia, from the moment her own family women bathed and spread holud over her at home, she could do nothing for herself. At her husband's home, her new female in-laws helped her with everything: they led her to the latrine, changed her clothes, and no doubt even blew her nose for her if necessary. When senior kinsmen came to visit, the women helped her to her feet and pushed her gently to the ground, so that she should touch their feet respectfully. She never spoke, and covered her face with her sari as much as possible.

I was to see many brides before I began to realise that this display, though partly a genuine expression of the fear and grief that I had seen in their faces, was also an age-old way for a girl to demonstrate that she had been well brought up, and would do her duty as a wife. Her averted eyes and covered face assure her new family that she will be obedient and knows her place – behind the veil of Islam, and at her husband's feet. She is the personification of sharom.

Sharom, the village women explained to me, is what you feel when a strange man catches sight of you; it is what you feel if your marriage is mentioned; it is the reason for covering your head, and not letting your sari rise up above your heels; it is why you hide behind your mosquito net if male guests arrive, and almost die of mortification if anyone sees the stains of menstrual blood on your sari. Shame, I soon learnt, was seen as part and parcel of being a woman.

Hand in hand with this in-built shame is the state of *purdah*, the veil. For the women whose families can afford for them not to go out in search of work, purdah means a shielding from strange men, a life spent rushing for cover whenever a man who isn't a relative or close neighbour appears. It was normal for the family women suddenly to fix their eyes upon the distant horizon and exclaim: 'Who's that?' as we sat chatting out in the yard or at the pond. Far off, across the fields, a male figure would be making his way along the path to the bari.

'It's Alim Ullah.'

'No, it's a stranger. Come in.'

And they'd cover their heads and hurry back inside, or to the back of the homestead, which was always the women's territory. After a few months, I was behaving in exactly the same way.

Purdah means that the lives of the village women are physically very closed. The richer ones have been to Sylhet, and a couple to Dhaka, but no woman would ever travel alone. Even if she is just going to the next village, she always takes at least a child with her. Some have never been further than the distance between their husband's and father's villages. For months on end, they stay on their bari; their world is the house, the yard and the pond. They might visit female friends and kin in the village, but the young wives of village men often come from outside, and therefore have none. Once or twice a year, they are taken home to their father's bari for a visit. A question that I was always asked whenever I was on a journey outside the village was: 'Are you alone?' After about six months of this I began to dread the question, and hate telling my travelling companions that yes, I was, and seeing the shock in their eyes.

All the women who could afford it in Talukpur had a burqua. Many of the younger ones had theirs in pretty shades of pink or cream, with frills at the cuffs or down the buttons at the front. 'Isn't it lovely?' I was often asked, as this garment was produced for my admiration. I could only ever smile weakly and say, 'But don't you feel hot in it?' Even in the winter, a walk at midday is a sweaty affair. In the summer, when by 7 a.m. the sweat is pouring off most people, to go out with a burqua over the top of a sari must be torture. After seeing the per-spiration dripping from exhausted women visitors who had walked to our bari in their burquas, and the speed with which they tore them off once safely in the confines of the building, I decided that this was one garment I would not try.

It was quite useless for me to question the state of purdah, just as it was useless to query the natural superiority of men, which everyone assured me of, for these beliefs were the very bindings of village culture.

'You say that women aren't as good as men, isn't that right? In my home, we say that we're equal. We believe that women and men are the same. We don't cover ourselves. We can go out if we want ... we're free,' I used to declare to any woman who would listen, hoping, in my first months of naivity, that they would eagerly accept my notions of liberation, and confide their hatred of their subservience with glee. Not so.

'Yah Allah, Beti, you have much to learn,' the more patient ones replied. 'Isn't it so that Allah made us this way? Of course men are more powerful than women. That is the way our God created it. If you don't cover your head and go around like a man, then you will be punished.'

'But look at me! I'm not a man, but I've come here, and I can study at college.'

'Your ways are different. So. But *we* say that there are two paths in life, that we must choose. One is white and pure, the other is covered with thorns that make your feet bleed. The first way is our Islam. We cover our heads and hide ourselves from men, and Allah is pleased. The other way – the women go in skirts, and show themselves like in your country, and those who take that path burn in hell.'

'So I'll burn in hell?'

'In your country it's different. Your women are just the same as men. But here, you follow our ways.'

Everyone was always too polite to admit that since I continually resisted their pleas to convert to Islam, hell was undoubtedly where I would end up.

On other occasions, I tried to ask why it was that women should follow such rules: 'But why did Allah make it like that?'

'Because it's good. It's our custom.'

'But don't you want more freedom?'

'Listen – we have men to care for us. We have brothers, and fathers and our husbands. That is their duty – so why should we want freedom?'

Any thought of sisterly consciousness-raising was rapidly revealing itself as a patronising and hopeless proposition. Anyway, I was slowly beginning to understand that what the women said they believed was not always the same as how they really saw themselves. I was being presented with an ideal, which the women did not wish to question openly but knew was often far from the truth. After all, if it was all so perfect, why were there abandoned and destitute women who begged from village to village? Everyone knew, too, that women often held the baris together, and were by no means less intelligent than men.

'More powerful than us, but not more intelligent,' older women would sometimes declare, with sly smiles.

The young brides might have appeared shrinking violets to my uninitiated eyes, but the older women were clearly of a different ilk.

'He does nothing, just pray!' Amma snapped one day, when I asked why it was she, not Abba, who was negotiating the sale of some of the family land. 'I'm just a woman, but haven't you seen how people respect me?'

It was during this period of weddings, new brides, and increasingly warm days and clear skies that I learnt of something which made me think even more carefully about the women whose lives I was sharing. One morning I visited Kudi Bibi's house, to find Sufia not, as usual, busy in the kitchen, but in the small dark room where she slept. She was lying on her bedding, and staring out into the dimness. I pulled myself up on to the wooden boards of the vast bed, bringing my feet off the earth floor and crossing them.

'What are you doing, Elder Sister?' I reached across and touched her shoulder, but she didn't even smile at my joking term for her. Instead she turned away and closed her eyes, and I saw that great tears were running down her cheeks.

'Sufia! What is it?'

There was a long pause, and then she sat up and faced me. 'Katy, do you remember me asking you to visit the bari of my mother-in-law?'

'Of course.'

'And did she show you affection?'

'Yes, I told you all about it.'

I had been visiting in the village where Sufia's in-laws lived the week before, and as a favour I had paid a call on their household. On my return Sufia had cross-questioned me exhaustively about what I had been fed, what topics we had discussed, and whether her mother-in-law had asked questions about Sufia and her family.

'But she did not speak about her bride – me – did she?'

'No.'

'Katy, there is much you don't know. She is a bad, bad woman. There are many things I haven't told you. Yah Allah – why should you want to hear of my griefs?'

'Tell me.'

'He isn't coming back.'

'Who?'

'My husband. He isn't coming back. You have lost your brother-in-law, it's all over.'

'What ... ? Who ... ? Is she crying?'

Banessa, her eyes popping with curiosity, had suddenly appeared. I had passed her on the path as I walked to the bari, and now she was standing in front of the bed, breathing a mixture of pan and chewing tobacco over us.

'No one. Nothing. Go away, Banessa.'

'Is it her husband? Doesn't he send you letters, Elder Sister?'

'Banessa, you talk too much – go!'

But Sufia, having had enough, had turned her back to us again, pulling the furled-up mosquito net above her down to create a shield from the room outside. It was the only fragment of privacy she had.

Later that day, after I had eaten my rice and was myself curled up inside my net with a book, relishing every moment of my escape, Sufia crept into my room and sat down quietly in the chair facing my bed. She often visited us in the evenings and we would talk until late, as the crickets chirped outside and Abba made his hookah gurgle in the next room. Tonight she was sharing Najma's bed, for Kudi Bibi had gone visiting relatives in another village and her household was empty.

'Are you working?' she asked. Everyone always thought that whenever I was reading, this, by definition, must be gruellingly hard work. 'Have you been to the ghat yet? The night is clear under the moon, and there's no one else there.'

So we went down to the cool stone steps and sat looking up at the stars. I knew Sufia wanted to tell me about what had been upsetting her.

'Why were you crying this morning?'

'Ai, what sadnesses I have!' She sighed heavily, and pulled her feet up underneath her. I could see that her eyes were filling with tears again.

'Can't you tell me?'

'Katy, I don't think my husband will ever come back here.'

'But he has to come back from Kuwait one day. How can he not?'

'He won't send for me again.'

'Yes, of course he will! Don't you think he cares for you?'

She said nothing. Was all this just because she hadn't received a letter from her husband for a couple of months? I had always semi-envied her security in knowing that he would eventually return, and was socially bound to care for her and not just wander off, or get someone new. In those first months in the village I had reckoned that the freedom and autonomy of the women around me had been traded in for some sort of security. The social rules which constricted them also in some ways protected them. I, on the other hand, had as much freedom as I wanted, but no assurance at all that I would one day have my own family. But I had also heard strange rumours about Sufia, and had never understood why women in other lineages always asked so avidly, 'Does the husband of that Sufia write to her? Why is she not at the bari of her mother-in-law?' and then exchange knowing glances with each other.

'Katy, I'm not welcome in the bari of my mother-in-law.'

'*What?*'

'You went visiting there, but she didn't ask about her bride, did she? She didn't send messages back to my sassa, or Ma. And she went to do Haj in Saudi with my husband just last month, but sent no word, or news to me, of how he was.'

It was true. On my visit I had been given the most lavish of receptions, but the shrivelled old widow who was Sufia's mother-in-law had not inquired how her daughter by marriage was, and something in her eyes had been cold and hard.

'When does she come to see me? She doesn't. When do my husband's younger brothers come to see me? They don't. They don't care for me. They say I am bad. They have told my husband that he must divorce me.'

'But why?'

'I don't know. Allah knows, not me. Yyshh ...

Out on the path leading into the village, a group of men were singing loudly as they walked home. We could see their lanterns moving slowly in the dark.

'She treated me so badly I had to come home. That's why I live here and not in my husband's village. From the very first she hated me, and said I wasn't good. Ma, I tried so hard. From the first day that they took me there, I did things only to please her. I worked from dawn to midnight, cleaning and cooking for her. My husband would tick me off, I used to work so hard. "Come and rest," he used to order me, "no more work, I forbid it". Every time there were guests I'd cook a special dish for them, and each day I'd prepare my mother-in-law's favourite sweetmeat for her. She'd just have to say, "I like it" and I'd make it for her. But she hated me. Every day she scolded me and wouldn't give me food ... '

'But didn't your husband do anything?'

'He only stayed a month after we were married – I have told it all to you before – and then he went off to Kuwait. "When you have our child," he said when he went, "then I shall stop working in Kuwait and come home to care for you" ... ' She did not need to finish, because I already knew that she had lost the baby many months before it was due to be born.

'They said it was my fault. My husband's brothers said I had lost the baby deliberately, out of spite. And he could do nothing, because he was abroad. Then they all wrote to him saying that I was bad, and he should break from me. I was very ill. All I could do was cry. I couldn't eat a thing – just a handful of rice at night – and I had a fever. No one spoke to me, they just left me alone to cry. Then one day my sassa heard what was happening, and he came to take me away. I haven't been back since then. That was six months before you arrived. Fourteen months now ... I have counted each day.'

'But Sufia, your husband still loves you.'

'No, he doesn't any more. His mother has told him many bad things about us. They said that if they'd known about our family – that we're not respectable enough – then they wouldn't have taken me. Now he writes and says that he loved me once, but now feels nothing. He has gone cold. But I have never turned cold for him! I remember every single moment that we were together. I think of him all the time.'

'What does he say to you in his letters?'

'Nothing. I don't know. I haven't had a letter for so long. He wrote two months ago that he no longer cares what happens. That he isn't going to come home. They plan for him to go and work in another country.'

'Perhaps if Abba went ... '

'What could he do? There is no one who can go. He can't – they'd insult him. Anyway, he is only my sassa. There isn't anyone who can help. My life is ruined, Katy.'

She stared mournfully out at the pond, with its hyacinths and lilies lit up in the moonlight. Above us, the palms of the betel nut trees moved reflectively on a breeze.

'Why didn't you tell me about this before?'

'I haven't talked to anyone about it. Who is there for me to talk to?'

'Not even Kudi Bibi?'

'She knows, but we don't talk about it.'

It was true. A young woman should not talk to her senior kinswomen about her marriage, as it is seen as a shameful topic, and to talk to senior male kin would be quite impossible.

But since no affairs are ever private, and all letters are read by everyone, it was unlikely that the rest of the lineage did not know what was going on.

'Every day I am alone with my sorrow. I laugh, and smile, but inside I know that my life has been ruined. You have not seen, but at nights, when everyone is asleep, I come out here alone. I can't find any peace. Everything is over for me.'

'But there must be something you can do ... '

'What is there? All I can do is pray. If Allah wished for my life to be destroyed, then I must accept it. That is the only way. If he doesn't come back then I shall die, I shall kill myself.'

'You can't!'

'I shall. What use would there be in carrying on living?'

'But isn't that a sin?'

'Maybe it is a sin, but then it must be that Allah wished me to sin, and go to hell.'

This left me temporarily speechless.

'But you're so young,' I said at last. 'You have to carry on. Can't you have another marriage? If this one ends, then can't you get another husband? A lot of people do that.'

'That may be what some women do, but I'm not like that. I only want to have one husband. We are a good family – no one has ever had a second husband before – not my aunt, or her mother, or any of my cousins. No. I accept my fate.'

And then we heard Kudi Bibi calling us to come and eat our rice, and the conversation was finished.

A few days later, Mobed came back from shopping at the bazaar with a letter. Everyone crowded round excitedly to see who it was from. It was in an airmail envelope, and covered in Kuwaiti stamps. Najma examined it carefully and declared it must be for Sufia.

'Go and take it to your auntie's bari, then!' she told Mobed, 'and make sure you find out what news there is!'

Later that day, Kudi Bibi came into my room and sat down on my bed. 'Katy, my niece,' she said softly, 'Sufia has had a letter from your brother-in-law.'

'Yes, I know. Is it good?'

'It's bad. Your sister has such sadnesses. Yyshh ... what worries I have! My head is hot from it all.'

'What's happening?'

'He writes to say she must take one path in life, and he another. What can we do? My girl is ill with grief. Such troubles we have!'

'Sassi, can't you find a better husband for Sufia? If she doesn't get married again, everything will be spoilt for her. There'll be no children.'

'What can I do? No one has done that before. And who is there to help us? Her father is dead, her uncles are sick and old and your brothers too young. Those cousins ... ' She leant across and whispered into my ear. I didn't understand.

'What?'

'I'm saying they're no good, that family of her mother. I would never trust them in this. If you ask me, they wrote bad things to Sufia's mother-in-law of our lineage, and that's why all this has happened.'

I had already heard vague talk of bad feeling between Sufia's maternal relatives and her father's family. There had been a dispute over the inheritance of land at her father's death, and it had never been properly resolved. They lived in the next village and, it was said, were a scheming lot.

'But what will happen to Sufia?'

'Allah knows, Beti, but there is one thing we can do.'

'What's that?'

'That *pir-saheb* [holy man] you were asking me about earlier, that one who we go to if we're sick and whose prayers can heal anything, you remember?'

I nodded agreement. I had been nagging Kudi Bibi to take me to see him for months, convinced that he would be able to teach me many things. She knew a great deal about the local healers, and would tell me far more about the Sufi pirs, who were not deemed religiously orthodox or respectable, than Amma or Abba.

'We can go to see him. In secret. If anyone hears, then we can say that we're going so that you can meet him – he's part of my lineage, you know. Then we can get him to give *jadhu*.'

'What's that?'

'Jadhu is what people with powers give. It's what we use if a husband doesn't care for his wife any more, and things like that. Do you follow me? So it's fixed? Acha I'll tell your abbe to bring us a boatman for tomorrow.'

I realised after Kudi Bibi had gone that the meaning of 'jadhu' was of course magic, and that we were actually going to the healer, or pir, or whatever people wished to call him, for a love charm.

The decrepit man lying on the bed in the centre of the room did not even twitch when we appeared, even though a large and noisy group of people had crowded in with us. Word had spread rapidly that a strange foreign woman had arrived at his bari, and it seemed that half the village had turned out to see her and find out what on earth she could be visiting the pir-saheb for. Instead, the 'small pir' (as men such as he were called) lay on his back with his eyes closed and his grimy prayer cap pulled skew-whiff over his face. He radiated neither mystic power nor spirituality, but simply shabbiness. I realised that if he was indeed related to Kudi Bibi, he was obviously a poor cousin. She had not spoken of him with great reverence earlier – unlike the great pirs buried in Sylhet, or other living ones, who were famous throughout the district for their inner strength and healing powers.

'Sometimes I go to see him, and listen to him, and sometimes I don't,' she'd told me in the boat on the way to his village. 'He was said to be holy a long time ago. He followed a very famous guru in another district, and then took up his ways and came back here. Then, he used to do great things. He had visions in his dreams, and could cure someone just by blowing on to them. but then ... you've heard what happened? He proclaimed that he had a message from Allah when his death would come, so everyone from all the villages round here, all his followers, went to his bari on the day that he'd said, to see his death. I went too. Ma, there were so many people there! Some even had spades so that they could dig his grave ready for his body. Everyone waited. "I'm about to die!" he told us all. We waited. And what happened? The beta didn't die. He kept closing his eyes, but we could all see that he was breathing. So now no one really believes in him. Not many people go to see him now, or sacrifice at the shrine of his guru in his bari.'

'So why do you want to go and see him today, then?'

'Well, Niece, it's just that I don't believe he's a great pir. But he can still give foo [blowing on somebody to heal them] and jadhu, can't he? That's from his knowledge, because he's read the Qur'an and knows so much, and he can't ever lose that. But it's true, some people do say he's a fake. Anyway, he's my cousin, isn't he?'

Kudi Bibi and I were placed on wooden chairs and sat facing the man, who occasionally groaned slightly. Perhaps he was in a trance, but more probably he was dozing. Everyone fell silent, waiting for him to open his eyes. Eventually Kudi Bibi, who never had much patience with bad manners, leant over him and said, 'Eh, Cousin, wake up.'

He gave a start and, moaning in complaint, slowly sat up to face us.

'Who's she?' he said abruptly, motioning at me.

'My English niece. She's living with my brother's family. She's trying to learn about our village life, so I've brought her to see you.'

'Eh? What for? What's she doing?'

'I say she's learning, Cousin. About our religion, and our Allah, and ... things.'

'Is she a Muslim?'

Kudi Bibi paused. This was something of a sore point, since all her and Amma's fervent attempts to convert me to Islam had so far failed. 'No.'

'Then the woman can't learn a thing. Go away and leave me in peace. There's nothing I can do for her. I need rest these days. I'm always sick.'

I was beginning to regret ever having come, and wondered very much how this shambles of a man, who could hardly be said to radiate spirituality, could help Sufia. Images of the faded fame and repute of rock stars, and their subsequent degeneration, drifted into my mind and stayed there.

'We've brought you an offering, Pir-Saheb.' Kudi Bibi placed on his bed the slightly crushed packet of biscuits that we'd sent Mobed to fetch from the bazaar.

'Pah! Biscuits! That's not enough! Now tell me what you want ...'

'Pir-Saheb ... an amulet?' And Kudi Bibi leant down and whispered something in her cousin's ear. He nodded in a bored way, then drew out a battered book from underneath his mattress. Leafing through it, he found the relevant section and screwed up his face in concentration as he read. Then he called for his family to bring him writing materials, and eventually, when everything was ready, began to scrawl words on a scrap of paper, which he folded and pushed at Kudi Bibi.

'Is it in Bangla?' I asked.

'You wouldn't understand,' the pir replied. 'No one can understand without learning such as mine! Now listen, Elder Sister, you can see how sick and weak I've become, so why don't you let me sleep some more?'

So Kudi Bibi secreted the amulet in her sari and, nodding at me to follow her, rose with more dignity than I had ever seen her demonstrate in the whole year I had known her. Two minutes later we were sitting with the pir's womenfolk drinking tea and discussing my sari and marriage prospects.

The amulet was given to Sufia in secret, after we'd returned. She took it in silence, knowing full well what it was and what it was for. She already had several others round her neck, for illness and to ward off evil spirits, like so many of the other village women and children. Kudi Bibi was careful not to let Abba or any of the other lineage seniors see, or find out that we had visited the pir-saheb for a love charm. They did not like the small-time holy men who claimed special powers from Allah, saying that such proclamations were heresy, and the use of magic was sinful.

'Sometimes the healing man gives medicines, too, to bring back men,' Sufia told me later. 'Then we put them into their food, and get them back with the powers of the potion. Other times they give amulets we put into their clothes. But how can I do that, since my husband is so far away?'

'And will it work?' I asked.

'If I believe in it, then of course. Everything you believe in, that you have faith in, works, doesn't it? So I shall wear it round my neck, and pray to Allah that my husband will love me again. Katy, in your country the women might always be jumping from one man to the next and divorcing their husbands, and having this freedom that you keep telling me about, but here, in my country, when all I have are my beliefs and faith, what else can I do?'

And then, since it was four o'clock once more and the azan had begun, Sufia pulled her sari over her head and went inside to pray.

5 THE LIVES THAT ALLAH TAKES

It was in the month of *Ramadan* that Shazna died. Hushnia had been married for a whole month, the fields lay empty of paddy and baking in the sun, and the final lingering traces of winter cool had finally evaporated, leaving the village in the first ferocious blasts of summer heat.

The fasting had been under way for two weeks now, and most people were exhausted. Only the very young or the very ill were exempt, and the rest had to make do as best they could without food or water through the long hours of daylight. I too was keeping the fast. Amma had tried at first to dissuade me from joining it, but I knew that it was perhaps the best public relations exercise possible, short of actually converting to Islam, which I had decided I did not wish to do. Everywhere I went, people asked, 'Are you fasting?' and when I told them yes, I was, and I also rose with the rest of the family at 2.30 a.m. to fill myself with cold rice before the dawn azan signalled the start of another day empty of food or drink, they were visibly pleased. Only the most probing asked, 'So, you keep our fast, but say you won't become a Muslim. What's the point in that?'

After getting up at dawn, we'd collapse again until the sun became too hot for sleep. The days seemed endless. By late afternoon everyone waited only for the moment when the sun disappeared and the dusk call to prayer brought release in the shape of the end-of-fast *eefta* meal. People fell thankfully on to their food, and after they had filled their bellies and satisfied their thirsts, there was an atmosphere almost of festival.

But even when it was dark, many villagers did not attempt to sleep, for although the sun had gone, the heat was stifling. Instead, they sat out on their verandahs or in their yards looking up at the stars and talking, against a background of squeaking *paka* fans and singing frogs.

I usually attempted sleep, the desire to shut myself away and switch off being stronger than the desire for some fresh air. But it was invariably hopeless. Inside my mosquito net it was suffocating and I would wake every half hour or so, my pillow damp with sweat. Then I would crawl outside to find Amma and Saleya still sitting on the verandah steps, chewing betel and talking quietly.

During the days, when the air felt as if it had come straight from an oven, the only place which provided any comfort were the mud floors. In the afternoon bodies lay scattered on mats as the flies buzzed and toads and lizards peeped out at them from the crannies in the rough walls.

It was during one of those long slow afternoons that the child was killed. Some people were sleeping, while others went wearily about their tasks. The village appeared to be an idyll of peaceful tranquillity, with its scattered baris, the wisps of smoke rising up from their thatch and tin roofs, the cry of birds, and occasional shouts of children as they played on the paths. The sun had just started its late-afternoon descent and some families had already begun to prepare the eefta meal. Many people were praying, with the familiar and comforting gestures of the worship with which they structured the day. Amma was crouched over her da, scaling a giant fish which Mobed had brought proudly from the bazaar; Najma and Bebi were working silently over the clay fires in the kitchen; and Abba was snoring on his bed. I was sitting in the yard, willing the sun to move more quickly across the sky, and hurry up and set.

And then suddenly a great roar of voices exploded the calm. Everyone on the bari began to shout that something had happened, something terrible – no one knew what – and that we should all run quickly to wherever it was, to see.

'Hurry, hurry!' Najma cried, running from the pond.

A distant sound of shouts and screams was coming from across the fields.

'What's happened? Oh, Ma, come faster – it's over there – Yallah, what's happened?'

Everything was abandoned. The piles of fish were left still twitching in the dirt, the children ran from their games and adults from their prayers. Out across the fields were the figures of people running from all directions towards the sound of shouting. It was coming from the largest and most prosperous of the baris, that of Tajmul Khan, Amma's uncle and one of the eldest of the elders, who now spent his days sitting in the yard looking out at his fields. There were nine households spread out in a line, all sharing a huge pond with an ornamental stone ghat, surrounded by an elegant row of betel and coconut trees. As people sharing blood with their lineage stumbled across the caked mud of the ploughed land, they called out to each other.

'What is it? Who? Who?'

'Shelly's child,' someone was saying.

'Oh dear God, Shazna, our little Shazna … '

I struggled to keep up, but was not so adept as the other women at keeping my sari intact as I ran, so I was soon left behind. I hesitated, too, for I feared that I was rushing to the scene of what was undoubtedly some family tragedy, where I could do nothing and would only be a voyeur. But as I was to learn many times over, one's presence at such moments is appreciated, not censured. To show interest is to show that one cares, and to turn a stonily blind eye, as I had been taught to do in Britain, demonstrates a cold heart.

When I reached the bari there was already a large crowd in the yard. A huge group of people surrounded Mustak Meer, one of the bari men, who was swinging something around over his head. As I got nearer, I could see that it was a little girl. From the buildings came a dreadful wailing, and many of the women, still breathless from their run across the fields, disappeared inside.

Kudi Bibi rushed past the crowd, not caring that her head was bare in front of so many men, and her usually neat bun a wild mess. 'Shazna, oh Shazna! Oh Mother, what are we to do?' she was crying. 'Drowned in the pond while her mother sat gossiping, drowned!'

Another man had now taken over from Mustak Meer. He held the child's body over his head and turned round and round, trying to bring air back into her lungs. They were arguing over who should try next, while the women stood clutching each other on the edge of the group.

It had happened before, and it would probably happen again. With so much water around, and so much time spent bathing, and washing, and playing in the bari ponds, it was inevitable that there would be accidents. Had not the married daughter of Abdul Mannen lost her child in exactly the same way? The village women knew the dangers all too well. They usually kept keen eyes on their children, and many of them still gave offerings to the Great Kwaz, saint of water, who watched over their safety. Stories told how he caught and saved children who fell into the grey deepness of the rivers, lakes and small ponds which filled the country, and because of this many mothers still included him in their prayers, even if the men laughed at them for their superstition.

But those hands which should lift children out and lay them down on the dry banks had not stirred when Shazna had fallen into the pond. Kwaz had not upset the calm surface of the water with its cover of water lilies and hyacinths. The only disturbance was in one corner near the slippery stone steps which led down to the water, where there had been some small splashes, but they had not lasted long and were soon replaced by spreading rings which scudded outwards until they shrank and finally disappeared. Shazna's playmate, her little two-year-old cousin, soon grew bored with crawling on the steps, and an older brother who had spotted him climbing back picked him up and carried him inside.

It was Lefus Meer, one of the bari labourers, who found the child. He had been working hard in the garden round the pond, cutting back the mango trees and clearing land to make a small vegetable plot, and had come down to the water to wash the soil from his hands. At first he did not understand what it was that was caught in the tangle of hyacinths; he thought it must be some animal which had stumbled into the water. Then he realised that he was looking at the body of a child. He flung himself towards it and, scooping it out of the water, ran with great bounding steps back towards the bari buildings.

And now the child's limp body lay in the dusty yard while the crowd stood around it. I hung back, for once willingly covering my head with my sari, feeling a horrified hollowness at what I was seeing. Only the day before I had visited Shelly, been given some glass bangles by her, and promised to come back and take Shazna's photo. I had also never seen a dead body before.

'Oh Ma! The little baby is dead!' Amma had suddenly appeared by my side, and was taking my arm as the tears poured down her face. 'My precious one! How many times haven't my own little ones died? How many times must we put them under the ground? Ma! Allah takes so many lives! Little Shazna ... '

Around us people were still arriving. The village Chairman's motorbike appeared, and he strode purposefully to the scene, but of course there was nothing he could do. Next came the village doctor, a plump young man who held a diploma in medicine from Sylhet and sold Western drugs from a stall in the tiny village bazaar. When people saw him a ripple of expectation spread through the crowd, for with his trousers and important-looking briefcase he possessed an air of authority and officialdom which would surely bring results.

They put Shazna's small body down on the dusty ground, and he examined her. Her eyes were closed, and she seemed to be asleep. Apart from the wetness of her hair and a scrap of vomit across her mouth, it was hard to imagine that anything was wrong. But the doctor shook his head and, after a pause, pronounced that there was nothing he could do and they must take her to the government medical post three miles away. The Chairman gathered her up in a bundle, and leapt again on to his Honda. As he started it up Shelly came running from inside, the crowd parting for her with the awe and respect that everywhere belongs to a woman who has just lost her child. She was screaming and wailing, her hair hanging limp and damp around her face. Her only child, and how she had loved her! How many times had she not sat with the toddler at her breast while her husband lay on the bed smoking and watching them both with calm joy? Only the week before they had come from his village for her cousin's wedding, Shelly in her burqua and her husband in his best punjabi, carrying their child over the fields. Shelly's eyes always gleamed with happiness; she still had the bright beauty of so many of the young village women, and a reputation for talking and laughing incessantly. Some of the older women thought her just a little too lively. Now, as the motorbike disappeared in a cloud of dust, she fell down and beat her head on the ground until female hands pulled her up and swept her back inside.

Shazna was buried the next day. The evening before they had laid her on a wooden bed in the centre of the room, covering the three-year-old's body with a cloth and burning incense around it. Her aunts and cousins had kept watch all night. Now it was morning, and visitors were arriving for one last look at her. In the corner Shelly's grandmother, a tiny shrivelled old lady with no remaining teeth, was reading the Qur'an, muttering the Arabic in a slow and broken voice. Shelly was lying sprawled on the floor in the next room asleep, or at least partially so, at last. People talked quietly around her, knowing what horror she would wake up to. Her husband too was sleeping. He had cried as much as his young wife, and his in-laws had been forced to physically guide him through the actions of his evening prayers.

'You must pray,' they had said as he sobbed and clung to them. 'It is your duty. You must pray for your little daughter's soul.'

All the lineage women had come, and many of their village neighbours. They sighed as they saw the child's body and her face was uncovered for them. Some sat for hours looking at it as the tears ran down their cheeks.

'Ah, the poor little one,' they said. 'Allah has decided to take her from us. She will go to heaven, that little one who was too young ever to sin. She'd pray there for her mother and father who are suffering so much; she'll look after them.'

They spoke of their own dead children too, the ones who had been taken by fever or diarrhoea. 'Allah ordered that I should lose four babies,' some said, wiping their faces with their saris. 'How much suffering there is in this world!'

The men kept away. On the other side of the bari some labourers had started to prepare the child's *palki* (death casket) by tying bamboo sticks together until a small platform had been built. Later they would place the body on this and carry it on their shoulders to the burial ground.

But first Shazna had to be cleaned, and Shelly's aunts carried her outside. They laid the body on a table, hung a mosquito net from poles around it to hide the sight of the laying-out from others' eyes, and burnt incense to hide the smell, for it was midday now, and the sun shone with an angry white light. Then they washed her, and pushed rags into her nostrils, as the others stood around watching and crying. The men had already assembled on the other side of the cowsheds which marked the entrance to the bari. There weren't many, just those of the Khan lineage, and the mullah. Since the child's death, a message had been sent to her father's own village some twenty miles away, but so far none of his kin had arrived and it was decided that the burial should proceed regardless. Already a large crowd of beggars had appeared. When a Muslim dies in Talukpur it is the tradition to distribute grains of rice or taka as alms to the local poor, to gain virtue for the departing soul and ease its entry into heaven. Shelly's uncles had gathered a huge basket of rice and moved up and down the rows of squatting children and women as they tipped a handful into the out-stretched bowls, banana leaves and rags of the destitute.

When the preparation of the body was finished, the women carried it over to the men. They followed it in a great huddle and peered from the cowshed as the mullah wrapped it in its white shroud and sprinkled perfume over it. The men hung back, in their best prayer caps and white punjabis, not looking in the direction of the women. Then they hoisted the palki on to their shoulders and carried it off to the graveyard, where it was forbidden for any woman ever to set foot, for this, like the mosque and the shrines scattered over the countryside, was a pure and holy place, and only men were allowed near it. Shelly, her hair hanging around her face and her sari loose and dishevelled, had been helped outside by her cousins. She was wailing, and as she watched the palki disappear with the men, she fell again to the ground whilst the rest of the women cried and fussed around her.

A few days later, I went with Amma to visit Shelly. I was, as usual, afraid of intruding, but Amma knew best.

'If you don't go, Shelly will think you don't care,' she told me firmly. 'If you go, everyone will see that you love her, and that you pray for her Shazna.'

So we tramped across the fields once more to what was now named temporarily 'bari of the death', where Amma had been born. She had put on her best sari and walked slowly, stopping every couple of minutes to peer at a clump of bushes and huts and ask, 'So whose bari is this?'

I could hardly believe it. Here was a woman who had never spent more than a week or so outside her village, yet still had difficulty naming all its baris or orientating herself.

'That's the bari of Alim Ullah, Amma.'

'Ah, I forget ... You spend so much time wandering around like a man that you know my village better than me!'

We found Shelly sitting on her bed, staring out of the window. To my relief, her face lit up when she saw me, but only for a tiny moment.

'So you've come! Did you see my little girl? Did you see her body? Did you see them put her in the earth? Will you pray for her?'

Amma, her duty to her niece done by showing her face – for physical presence is just as important in times of crisis as endless advice – had slipped off to the kitchens for a gossip with her aunt.

'My little girl is in heaven now. The angels took her. She is there ... looking after us ... ' Shelly went on. 'In your country, do you bury the dead too, or burn them like those Hindus? Yah Allah, and I don't even have her picture.' And she began to cry again.

A month later, Shazna was no longer mentioned. What, after all, was there to say? The family had to go back to normal, life had to go on. Children die in the villages of Bangladesh too often for public mourning to continue for very long. It is not that they are forgotten, or that their relatives do not grieve deeply; every family has its own dead children, its own small graves to remember and mourn when another household loses a child. And it certainly would be many months before Shelly would laugh naturally again, or not sit staring out across the bari speaking of her little girl. But her relatives did not worry too much; she was young, still under twenty, and from the bulge within the folds of her sari they realised that soon another baby would be coming to replace the one that had been lost. For just as Allah took lives, so He gave them.

6 ROUKEA BUYS A NEW SARI

One afternoon I came home to find everyone in the yard, talking animatedly and passing round a length of bright orange material whilst a figure squatted on the ground in the midst of them, crying. It was Roukea, the wife of a poor and distant cousin called Habib, who had been living on the bari since their own home had been battered down by the monsoon floods. They stayed in a small dark room at the back of the bari which had previously been occupied only by hens and several exceedingly large spiders. It had once been the household of one of Abba's brothers, but its dust and cobwebs now spoke only of its abandonment, and their long absence in Britain. Their small family was almost, but not quite, part of the bari now, and Roukea often came into my room to see me, or sit and listen to the talk of Amma and her kin.

'One hundred and fifty!' Amma was saying. 'Beti, I'm not surprised he gave you a hiding. You should have argued it down more.'

'You can get them cheaper in Sylhet. Yssh! It's not very good quality either. Don't cry, there's nothing you can do now. We don't want to buy it off you. Come and look, Katy, your stupid Roukea has bought a sari, but her husband doesn't have any money to pay for it, and now she's trying to sell it to us!' Sufia was laughing heartily at the comic situation. Much as I cared for her, sometimes her sense of humour was a complete anathema to me. Roukea sniffed loudly.

'You keep your new sari, Beti, some day your husband might decide you look pretty in it. Yah Allah, well, I've got work to do. Daughter, go and wash the rice.' Amma pushed the cloth into Roukea's hands and, muttering to herself, returned back up the verandah steps. Sufia, too, had lost interest and had gone down to the pond to cleanse herself for the afternoon prayer. Roukea was now carefully folding the material, smoothing it out lovingly, as her tears splashed on to it.

'It's very pretty,' I said. She usually wore a yellow sari so dilapidated that it hung limply around her ankles, and so stained and faded that its pattern was no longer visible. She smiled fleetingly at me, and then blew her nose out on to the dusty floor.

'Katy,' she said, looking up, 'do you have any money?'

'A little.'

'How much?'

'Roukea, is it for the sari?'

'The sari pedlar came, Ma, and he had such beautiful cloths, and so I chose one. I only have two saris, you've seen that, haven't you? And how both of them are rags. I've had them for years, I haven't bought a new one for so long. I don't even have a blouse, and no petticoat either. What am I to do if I want to go out visiting? How can I go back to my father's bari, looking so poor?'

'I don't know, Roukea.'

'How much money have you got? Can you lend me one hundred taka? I'll be able to pay you back at the end of the month, I'll find someone else to lend it then.'

'Sister, I can't buy you a sari. If I do that, I'll have to buy clothes for every poor woman in the village, and you know how many there are. Anyway, I need my money to go to Sylhet next week. I've lent the rest already to Amma ... Can't your husband get some money from somewhere?'

It was a stupid question.

'He can't,' Roukea replied, and then in a quiet voice she added: 'Abdul Sofan's father is very angry with me. He beat me, and said I was worthless, and he didn't want me as a wife.'

'Is that why you're crying?'

'He said he couldn't buy a fish from the bazaar for supper, let alone a sari for me. But I don't see why I must always look like a beggar! See – 'And she pulled her sari away from her shoulders to reveal great red and black bruises on the tops of her arms, and then more on her flanks.

'Does it hurt?' It had not taken me many months to pick up the village habit of asking stunningly obvious questions.

'Ma! I hurt all over. Do you have any of your medicine for it?'

'Come on, come into my room and I'll give you some antiseptic cream, if you think that'll make you feel better.'

And so we went inside and, except for Roukea and Habib, the subject of the new orange sari was forgotten.

Roukea and her small family had come to live on the bari many months ago now, one grey September morning in the very worst of the rains, on a day when only the most intrepid ventured into the soaking deluge outside. The pond had already spread over the top step, and for some time there had been talk of flooded baris and houses overtaken by the water. But we were lucky, for give or take the odd puddle, the insides of the buildings were still dry. It was during the empty lull between breakfast and preparations for the afternoon meal that the boat Habib had borrowed to move their small collection of belongings glided quietly into the slippery slope of land which had become the bari's own little port. Two small children appeared first, the eldest pulling his toddling sister behind him, whilst their father began to carry the basket containing their worldly goods towards the bari buildings. Roukea followed slowly behind, padding across the wet yard with a tiny bundle of baby in her arms. I already knew them; their hut was not far away, out in the fields on the edge of the village, and I had visited it many times to sit with Roukea and let her unruly children crawl over me.

'Habib and Roukea have come to live here,' Amma told me as we watched the boat arrive.

'To live?'

'Their bari's flooded. Totally destroyed. Didn't you hear the rain last night? So we're going to give them the room where your uncle once lived.'

'How long will they stay?'

'Allah knows, Beti. When the rains stop I suppose they'll build another hut. Now the water's up to here.' Amma pointed to her waist. 'You go and ask your Habib, he'll tell you. Hey, Roukea, come here – your sister Katy's asking after you.'

Roukea smiled surreptitiously at me as she squatted down next to Amma and put her child's mouth to her breast.

'Your bari's flooded?'

'It's the will of Allah. Nobody knows how much we suffer.' Roukea always talked like this, and I tended to ignore it.

'What happened?'

'It rained and bit by bit the water rose. Yesterday it came up to our ankles. Then that storm – you heard the rain? I lay awake all night listening and worrying that it would come in. Then at dawn, when the sun began to lighten the room, we saw that the water was right up to our knees, nearly over the top of the bed. Everything's gone. Ruined. What can we do?'

And so Habib and Roukea set up house in the bari. The water did eventually subside, but there was no money to buy materials for a new home, and as the months merged into each other, and the fields dried out, it became obvious that the poky dark room had become their new home, and they stayed.

Habib could barely have been over forty, yet his forehead was furrowed with the deep lines of a man who has known few comforts in his life. He was lean, wiry and tight with muscle, and had the sure feet of someone who has always used his body to earn his living. He never lost his step in the mud of the paddy as he ploughed, in the river-bed as he fished, or on the brow of one of the village's battered wooden boats, which he punted through the water as if it were an extension of himself. He worked in the household of Mohammed Meer, another distant cousin, when they needed him and could spare his wages.

Everybody called him 'Brother'. Even the young sons of Mohammed Meer, whom he had held in his arms when they were babies and carried on his hip to see their father's cows and fields before they could walk, called him that now, and had started to shout at him authoritatively when his work did not please them. For his part, he referred to Mohammed Meer as 'Uncle'. He had worked on his land for almost as long as he could remember, and now there was no one whom the old man trusted more than Habib, who knew every inch of his soil as if it were his own, and coaxed it like a baby to give high yields. Recently, as Mohammed Meer had grown older, he had taken to sending Habib out on his business, confident that at the bazaar he would always strike a good deal and get admirable prices for the grain that he was entrusted to sell. Mohammed Meer's wife never bothered to hide when he came inside to eat his rice, and would sometimes share her betel and pan with him as they sat out in the yard. Habib was as much a part of the bari as the aged dog that lay in the shade and snored as the flies buzzed around its muzzle.

He was not a great one for talk or the frivolity of many words, and perhaps that was why people trusted him. Sometimes he would speak

quietly of his problems: of the never-ending cycle of work and the
cost of buying food for his family, the loans he was forced to take,
and then the burden of paying back his debts. He took life seriously
and hard, and did not have time for dreaming of what it could have
been if he only had some land of his own. But he was sharp, and grasped
ideas with the same surety as he handled Mohammed Meer's plough.
He knew a great deal about the business of fields, and money, and
village affairs. Whenever a *panchayat* (village council) meeting was held
he would quietly slip in at the back to listen and learn so that one day,
if he ever needed it, he would have knowledge of village law. He had
never learnt to read, but Mohammed Meer had once taught him how
to form the letters of his name, and he had never forgotten.

Roukea had come to the village as Habib's wife about eight years
ago. She was barely adult when Habib and a few of his family men
had come for her at her father's bari, but now, three children on, the
early bloom of her beauty had passed away, and the early days of her
marriage had receded into the distant corners of her memory. With
the babies, her breasts and stomach had sagged, and her arms and legs
had grown thin. There had been more pregnancies, too, but the
ghosts had taken the children before they had even been named. She
tried to forget about those babies.

Sometimes Roukea cursed her fate. Her father had never been rich,
but before her marriage she had never known such poverty as this.
Her sisters all had husbands with some land, yet she had been given
to a man with nothing. Over the years she had absorbed Habib's
melancholy, but not his willingness to work, seeing life as a series of
events, usually bad, which Allah, or Habib, inflicted upon her. Like
the makeshift hut which now lay in ruins out in the fields, the small
room where they now lived remained uncleaned, and her children
ran amok whilst Roukea cradled her baby or wandered around the
bari silently staring at the family women with their lives full of cooking,
new saris, and village gossip. Sometimes they gave her old clothes or
let her use their hair oil whilst they muttered complaints about the
way her little Abdul Sofan ran around screaming and upsetting the
hens. The days were long and usually empty for Roukea as she waited
for Habib to return from the fields and prepared the little bit of food
she would give him for his supper.

Habib cared for her in his own way. It was right, he believed, that
he should have a woman to see to his needs and give him children to

carry on his line, however insignificant it may have seemed to outsiders. He wanted as many sons as possible, even if he had to scrape the bottom of the rice pot to feed them now, for they would bring in vital wages when they were older. Roukea felt differently, but never told her husband that she didn't want to spend her whole life swollen like a balloon or weak and deflated with a baby at her breast. She was only twenty-two now, but already felt middle-aged.

In the first days of their marriage, Roukea and Habib had stayed with his sister and her large family in their hut on the other side of the village. The sister's husband was also a labourer, and most of her children were grown-up, but even though several daughters had now married into different villages, there were still twelve of them. It was a busy and chaotic household, with continual visits from married daughters and their babies, and food stores that were rarely full enough to satisfy everyone's hunger regularly. Habib and Roukea slept on the floor in the area used during the day for cooking. In the hot wet season the damp seeped right into their bones, and in the winter Roukea caught a chill which nearly killed her. Eventually the quarrelling, which had spread into every nook of their lives, became too much, and with the help of his richer cousins and Mohammed Meer, Habib obtained enough money to buy the materials he needed to make a smart bamboo hut, and he built it within the land of his brother-in-law's cramped bari.

During those first years of her marriage Roukea had been afraid of her husband, for he was so much older, and so stern with her. Sometimes he had beaten her in silent fury for her laziness and the endless fights she was having with his sister over money and food. Once or twice he had even threatened to send her back to her father. But now he rarely showed his anger. Their new home mellowed him, Mohammed Meer had grown more prosperous and raised his wages – perhaps life was growing easier. At night I could sometimes hear the sounds of Habib singing for his family, his slow strong voice blending with those of the crickets and the frogs. He loved his children passionately, and if he didn't have to go out to work for Mohammed Meer he would take Abdul Sofan to the bazaar with him, or for visits to his village relatives. As I sat by the pond in the evenings waiting for the sun to set and the mosquitoes to gather, I often saw them coming back to the bari along the path which ran through Abba's fields, the little boy running in front and Habib striding behind, occasionally carrying a basket of rice or a bundle of sticks for Roukea's fire on his head. Sometimes he carried his small son, who had grown tired from the walking, in his arms.

Many hours after I had rubbed ointment into Roukea's bruises for her, Habib came into my room and sat down heavily on the chair. 'Sister,' he started, 'I'm in a lot of trouble. Can you lend me some money?'

'I really don't think so. Roukea asked me earlier.' I was already distinctly uneasy about my resolution never to give charity. But after seeing Roukea's bruises, I was also not exactly feeling over-warm towards Habib.

'I had one hundred taka saved for my son's medicine, for his bad chest, that the doctor said I should buy, so what should I do now? The sari was one hundred and fifty. She borrowed the money from Abdul Hossain, who's just got some from his father, but he must have it back by tomorrow. I've been to all my family's houses, but they all say that they've no cash. So I'll have to go to the moneylenders, and they charge twenty per cent interest. I work all year, and still there's nothing but debt!'

'Are you still very angry with my Roukea?'

'What's anger? What good is it? My wife is young, and doesn't know enough about life. If I could, I'd buy her saris of gold, but I can't. All there is to eat is rice, and you've eaten from our pot, even that isn't tasty – it isn't from my own land.'

He took a battered bedi from the folds of his lungi and lit it from my hurricane lamp. 'I wasn't born to this; you can put that down in that book you write in. My father had land.'

'He had some land? So what happened?'

'He died, Ma, when I was a baby, younger than Abdul Sofan. All I had was my mother and my big sister, who was already married here. So we lived in my mother's brother's bari, and then she died, so I came here to stay with my sister. Then, when I was older and had got to know the world a little, I realised that I should have some land from my father. So I went back to his village, to the bari of my uncles, and said to them, "My father died, leaving land for me to inherit when I get older; well, here I am, all grown up, so I'm making my claim." And my uncle looked at me, and said, "He didn't leave you any, boy.

We've taken it." He was lying, but I didn't have any papers to prove it. My mother had told me many times that he had left me his land, and why would he give it to his brothers and not his son? So then I tried to go to the *panchayat* and get them to help me, but they wouldn't. My uncle is a big man, and they were afraid he'd make trouble for them if they helped me, so all I could do was give up and come back here and get work. My uncle had said before that he would let me live on his bari, but I'm not his servant, and as God is my witness, I won't go back there until he gives me my rightful land. So now I have nothing, and since the flood took our house, even less than before. I work all day, every day, to feed my family. That's what Allah has willed for me, perhaps by next year He will have willed something else. But for today, what can I do? My wife has a fine new sari, but I'm broken.'

He threw the bedi on the floor and stood up. 'So you don't have any spare money?' He was eyeing the bag where he knew I kept my cash.

'Oh God, take it,' I said in English, and rummaging in the bag produced one hundred and fifty taka. Habib stuffed it into his lungi.

'I'll return this,' he said. 'I'm a poor man. My country is poor, and I'm at the bottom of the heap. But I know that if I just have faith, and wait, and trust in God, then us poor will be rewarded. If you have that belief, then you don't need fine clothes or food.'

And with these words Habib, broken man, believer, and today, a husband who had beaten his wife, returned to the small dark room where his children were sleeping and Roukea was draining the rice. She was working with special care today, once more beginning to hum to herself and making sure not to dirty her brand-new bright orange sari.

7 STORIES OF THE SPIRITS

It was in the week of *Eid* that I heard of a strange visitor who had come to one of the homesteads. The village had greeted the end-of-fast festival with great relief, but although thirsts could now be quenched, the days grew steadily hotter. I began to feel as if I were living in a furnace. 'Yallah, so much heat!' people cried as they saw me. 'Is it hot like this in London?'

The worst fate of all in such weather was to come out in a prickly heat rash. These plagued many people during the hottest months, and often became infected, turning into angry, painful boils. It was not uncommon for the infection to lead to fever, and Bebi spent a whole week crying with pain and lying inside, because the boils on her leg were too painful for her to walk. I was more fortunate, and although I complained more than the rest of the village put together, I never once suffered from prickly heat. I spent vast amounts of time bathing in the pond, swimming into its scummy centre to get to cool water, and sleeping. But even sleep was a poor option, for I would wake covered in sweat and hideously bad-tempered.

It was on a day like this that I met a little girl hurrying along the small paths that ran between the paddy towards one of the richest baris in the village.

'Are you coming to see, Elder Sister?' she shouted out at me.

'See what?'

'This man has come, and there's this ghost there, and everyone's gone to see ... '

I didn't have a clue what she was talking about, but followed her all the same.

By the time we reached the bari, everything that might have happened was over. There was a small crowd of men standing under the homestead's fruit trees and talking, but nothing else. I found Jamilla Khatun, a venerable lady in her sixties with a tiny, shrivelled body but the loudest of voices, shredding bamboo in her back yard.

'Oh Ma! What can I say?' she cried when she saw me. 'Today it's all over, but yesterday, what excitement there was! All this has been sent to us by Allah; we cannot understand such things. Come inside – Daughter, make the foreign beti some tea – and I'll tell you what happened.'

'Listen, Golden Ma, I'm going to tell this just how I saw it.' Jamilla Khatun perched on her bed and sucked at an enormous hookah as her keen eyes glinted at her audience. As she spoke her youngest daughter turned a large bamboo fan, which wafted the warm air in gentle gusts and squeaked comfortingly. I could feel the now familiar sensation of sweat running down my back.

'It happened yesterday,' she said, and with sighs of delight the grandchildren around her moved a little closer and laid their hands on her knees. They had already heard the story many times before, but loved to hear it again, and later, at the small village school, would tell it themselves, for they too had seen what she was about to describe with their own eyes.

Their grandmother paused and the hookah bubbled again. Nobody dared make a sound. She had tremendous authority in the household, and her daughters-in-law cowered under the sharpness of her tongue. They were the richest family in the village, with their own private mosque and a large brick bari painted white and pink, with flower designs right up to the tin roof. Jamilla Khatun had been head of the family for many years now, since her husband had died, and she ruled her household and sons with a firm hand.

'How many ghosts do not come to our country?' she began. 'Ma! How many evil spirits are not carried on the winds? You must take such care. You go wandering around outside with your head uncovered, and you'll be caught. They'll pull you up by your hair, and you'll become quite mad. Some have died – haven't you ever heard of it? Look at that ... what's his name?'

She inclined her head slightly in the direction of one of her neighbour's baris. 'That daughter of Jamil Ahmed Meer. She was possessed for months. Oh, how she wandered around the village with all her sari loose and her hair hanging down, until they had to tie her to her bed with chains to stop her from going out and shaming them any more! She spoke so much, so many mad words, and no mullah could force the ghost away. Now you see her, and she says nothing. Yallah, what griefs her mother's had! They'll never be able to give her away in marriage ... '

It was true. Although to the casual observer nothing could seem safer than a Bangladeshi village, it does in fact contain great dangers for the unwary. I had not been in Talukpur long before I realised that the family's continuous urgings that I should always cover my head and never, whatever the circumstances, walk alone at night were less to do with the feminine modesty which I so blatantly lacked, and more to do with fear of evil spirits or ghosts [*bhut*]. 'Evil spirits of the winds!' Amma often said when I asked why someone had fallen sick. 'The child was caught by *bhut*.'

All children, and many adults in the village wore amulets to protect them from these malevolent spirits which could so easily take their lives, and most households hung Arabic writings over doorways to prevent them from entering. There were complicated rules surrounding these, which I often unknowingly broke. After attending a funeral, for example, I had to bathe thoroughly before going inside the bari building. Failure to do this, everyone assured me, would destroy the power of the amulets over the doors.

'So a bhut came to your bari, Aunt?' I asked. Like the children, I loved to hear about ghosts.

'Listen, Beti, I shall tell it all.'

Two women in the thin green saris of destitution slipped into the room and squatted on their heels. They had been pounding rice into powder all morning and, their work finished, had come for their wages, but they always had time for a story.

'And Kameran too!' a grandson interrupted. 'Kameran was caught by bhut too!'

He was right. The young son of a poor cousin had been lying in their small hut for several weeks now, stretched out in a stupor. Only the flicker of his eyelids showed there was any life in him, and his mother sat over his bed and wrung her hands whilst a succession of mullahs and *kobiraj* (traditional healers) came and went, all failing to make contact with the malevolent spirit at the root of the boy's sickness. They supposed he had been caught whilst walking home late at night by the river path, which was overhung with huge ancient trees. Everyone knew that bhut often made their homes in the wilderness and trees, and in the places of filth: the latrines and cesspits on the edges of the baris were also dangerous. Everywhere lonely or dirty should be avoided. The villagers hardly ever slept alone, and were horrified when they heard that I actually preferred not to share my bed with the family women.

'But aren't you *afraid*?' I was asked so many times that I eventually began to wonder if perhaps they weren't right, and I wasn't rather odd.

People were also careful not to walk alone at the particularly dangerous times of the night – between the last call to prayer and the first one at dawn. There were many stories of people who had been led astray by the lamps of bhut, and had spent hours wandering in confusion until eventually light came and they found themselves many miles from their destination. This type of spirit appeared as glow-moths at dusk, but turned into the forms of men in the dark.

But who could generalise about bhut? Were there not as many types of spirit as there were of people?

'Nobody is sure that it's a bhut that has made Kameran sick, Grandchild,' Jamilla Khatun said. 'How can we tell why Allah sends such things?'

Nevertheless, whenever one of the villagers became mysteriously ill or crazy, most people explained it in terms of bhut. Take Fesi. It was impossible to know her age, although she looked at least fifty, for she had spent so many years as Talukpur's madwoman, sleeping out in the open and eating scraps, that her face was prematurely marked by deep lines and she had lost all her teeth. She would go hobbling from bari to bari, a small bent figure with a ragged sari, a shaven head (for it was believed that a cause of sickness and madness was overheating of the head, and therefore by cutting the hair, the sufferer would be cooled) and a begging bowl, and then sit wailing in the yard until she was chased away. The village children took great pleasure in bullying her, hitting her with sticks and surrounding and prodding her until she started to cry. Her greatest trick, for which she was famous, was her penchant for taking off her sari, until with hoots of laughter and cries of horror any women nearby got to her and covered up all her offending parts.

Fesi had been caught by a bhut many years ago. Some people said she was a Hindu who converted to Islam; she was certainly once married and then probably abandoned, and once had children, although they were all dead now. The villagers did not let her starve and she was given shelter, whenever she chose to take it, in the home of a widow who had a few ducks and just enough money to make it possible for her to spare the occasional bowl of rice.

Another woman wandered from village to village with her hair loose and her sari hanging open. She was far younger than Fesi, probably no more than twenty, and men eyed her with surprised curiosity as she passed. She never spoke, but something in her eyes, which didn't avert themselves from the men's gaze, and the angle at which she held her battered brolly – far too high over her head, as if it were an effort to stop it from flying away – made it plain that she too had been a victim of bhut. Spirit possession really was very common.

But what had happened on Jamilla Khatun's bari was more sensational than someone simply becoming crazy. It was to be the talk of the village for days, and many people, on hearing that something strange had happened, had come rushing over to see. The tale which Jamilla Khatun was relating was more than a product of her great talent for storytelling.

'It was midday,' she began, 'and I was sitting in here. Then in comes our cowherder and says, "Oh Nanazie [Grandmother], come and see what's happening outside." So out I went with him. And there ... Oo, over there in that tall tree at the back of the pond, I saw a man. There he was, sitting in the branches all hunched up in this way, like an eagle.'

She hugged her knees with her thin arms. '*Kha! Kha! Kha!* went the crows around him. *Kha! Kha! Kha!* Well, what was I to do? I looked up at him from this way, and then that, and he carried on sitting up there as if he wasn't human at all. But he was a respectable type. Shirt, clean lungi, good sandals. About twenty-five, I'd say.'

She paused, but no one moved. Outside, the distant cries of the midday azan hung on the air, and she put her hand up to her head to pull her sari more closely over it. The poor women squatting in the corner followed her gesture and reached for more pan.

'This happened today, Nani?' one of them asked.

'No, Woman! Yesterday, that's when it was. Oh, such heat – the sun like fire. Well, what could I do? So I went back in, as that sun was making my head spin, and waited. Afternoon came, and we ate our rice. Then the cow lad comes back. "Nanazie" he says, "come now and see what he's doing." A big crowd had gathered by then. Yallah – so many people, right up to the trees over there, and the fields to the other side. My eldest sons aren't here, of course, and I am left alone. Only those wives in the kitchen and my son Koddus Meer, who does nothing but lie around all day and smoke.'

She began to sniff, remembering her husband, who had lain in his grave under the great tree at the edge of the bari for so many years, and the other sons who had now migrated to Britain and came back only every five years or so. The youngest son had recently been married off, but this had not increased his sense of responsibility. He was a sickly fellow with great protruding eyes and a high-pitched giggle, who enjoyed visiting his relatives and being fed sweetmeats, and avoided becoming involved in anything remotely resembling work. Everyone knew that when it came to the business of land, or labourers, or the bari, it was Jamilla Khatun who pulled the strings.

'So what happened, Aunt?'

'Aren't I telling you, child?' The old woman delicately blew her nose on to the floor, and continued: 'I didn't like to go out in front of all those men, but I knew I had to see what was going on there. It's not like your country here, we can't go wandering around like men, with our bodies on show.' She looked at me reprovingly. 'Cover your head, and Allah will be pleased.'

I did as I was told, and she carried on.

'There were so many men there – so I pulled my sari right down over my face – you've seen a new bride? Like that – and went out to the tree. Ma! What a sight! That boy was still up there, but he was talking. Saying such words, and in such a beautiful language, like you've never heard. They'd brought him food, but he wouldn't take it. Everyone was standing round the tree just watching and listening. And even though the branches are only so thin, still he didn't fall.

"'Oh Ma! Oh Golden Ma!" he was crying. "Why can't you leave me? Why have you taken me up here into this tree? What destruction you've caused! My mother is blinded by her tears for me, tied to her bed in chains, she's so mad with grief!"

'And then he starts wailing, and crying out for water ... '

'Yallah!' the women whispered as they listened. 'Oh *Nanazie*, what kind of spirit was this?'

Jamilla Khatun turned to the gaunt women sitting by her feet. 'A *pori*,' she said. 'A pori who had caught him when he was only a child. He told me everything after he'd revived. What a tale!'

Poris are beautiful female spirits who live in trees and gardens, attracted by the smells of fruit and flowers. They seduce unwary men, tempting them with their fair skin and flirtatious ways and leaving them stunned and in a state of disarray after they have sated their lustful desires.

'She came to him and wanted to marry him. She forced him to lie with her until he was completely bewitched. When he told his family they all came to see the woman in his bed, but when he pulled back the covers they saw only a snake lying there.'

'But he saw a pori!' one of the children added.

'Yes, Granddaughter. They refused to give their son in marriage to a spirit, so she stole him away from them. That was how he told it.'

'She stole him away from them ... ' the poor women echoed.

'Oh Ma! How many times! She led him away, far into other countries, and he was like a madman and didn't know where he was. It was in that way that he came to our bari. His father's country is far away – Mymensingh. He couldn't remember a thing; all he knew was that he'd been led here by the pori. Sometimes when he was telling me his story he'd suddenly start wailing: "Oh Mother, Oh Sisters, Oh Brothers, what land have I come to? How can I return to you?" Another time, he told us, she'd taken him to her own country, to Poristan, and he'd stayed there for three years, eating only fruit. Everything's made of gold in Poristan, even the people. Then he returned to his mother and saw how she'd been broken with sorrow for her lost son.'

'So then what happened?'

'Nani, tell about how he came down.'

Jamilla Khatun pulled her grandson on to her lap and stroked his head. 'Little Uncle, can't you keep still? I shall tell it all just how I saw it.'

She paused, and then went on: 'And still he was up there. Eventually our *mehsahib* came, all in a hurry and excitement.

'"Where is he? Where is he?" he was saying.

'"Ooh ... Over there." We pointed to the tree.

'"I'll get my gun and shoot him down!" he was crying.

'"No, lad, don't do that, the only person you'll end up shooting is yourself," I told him.

'Then he rolled up his lungi, and started wading into the pond. "I'll throw stones, and that'll bring him down!" he said.

"'Oh Mehsahib! The only person you'll hit will be yourself!"

'And then, just at that moment, the mullah arrived. You have seen our mullah? Allah be praised, what a holy man! Next to him, that mehsahib of ours is just like a child. He walked over to the pond, looked over the water to the tree, and then pushed his walking stick deep into the ground. *Kha! Kha! Kha!* sang the crows. At that moment the lad fell down through the branches of the tree, but lightly, like a leaf. He crawled over to the pond and drank from it, like cattle at water, not using his hands but drinking it straight with his mouth. Then he collapsed. And there he lay. We thought he was dead. He was lying on his side with spit dribbling from his mouth. Well, we moved him into the shade and fed him water, and after a while he came round. That's when he told me his story.'

'Yallah!'

'And did the mullah cure him?' I asked.

'Oh, Ma – how he tried! We fed him up with rice and then our mullah-sahib tried to get rid of that pori. He said all manner of spells, blew his holy breaths on to him, read from our holy book, but nothing happened. Eventually the lad just came round and started to feel better, then said it was time to go home.'

'And he hasn't come back?'

'No, Ma, he hasn't returned yet. We don't know what happened. He said he'd come back to visit, but whether he will Allah knows. Actually, if you ask me, I'd say that pori will take him off on his wanderings again.'

'Yshh!'

'It's true, too! And then the man went back home. Abba gave him money and walked with him to the road. We all saw it!'

'Grandson, I've already said that. You're never quiet, always shouting and giving your *nani* a headache. Come on, child, off you go. I've had enough talking. I've got work to do. Tsh, what heat! Eat up those biscuits, girl! Fill your stomach and get fat!'

And then Jamilla Khatun slipped off her bed and padded out into the yard to turn the drying rice with her feet, glancing as she did so over to the branches of the tall mango tree where the pori had landed. It stretched effortlessly above the rest, its leaves pinkened by the late-afternoon sun, and its great shadow falling across the water of the pond.

Not long before this episode another possession had taken place in the village, and this too had been the subject of much talk for many

weeks. It concerned the young man who lodged in our bari and studied
at the small village madrasa. Many of the madrasa students came from
outside Talukpur and were put up and fed by local families pleased
to have a connection with such a holy institution, knowing that such
charity could only please Allah and bring His blessings to their homes.

The student was called Abdul Hossain, and he was an important
contact for me with the male world of the mosque and the madrasa.
In rural Bangladesh women are not allowed into such places, for, men
told me, their presence would not be seemly; they would be seen by
strange male eyes and, far worse, would distract the men from the holy
business of prayer.

Another reason, too indelicate to tell me, was that a woman's
natural functions make her impure. If she is menstruating, or has
recently given birth, she cannot pray, or even touch the Qur'an.
Even when she is not in these states the village women do not enter
the mosque. The reasons were explained to me by men through
vague allusions and obscure metaphors. Women put it far more simply:
'Isn't it so that you have your period? Well, that's a dirty business,
and no one who's dirty can go to our mosque.' Whatever the expla-
nation, as a woman, I was banned.

Abdul Hossain was a cheery boy of about seventeen, with the first
sproutings of a moustache on his lip and pimples on his chin. Although
he was shy of me at first, we soon became good friends and I often
visited him in the special room on the edge of the bari which was kept
for male guests so that they would not see the family women, and
listened to his fine rendition of saints' songs, or his explanations of Islamic
orthodoxies. I would always wake to the sound of him reading the
Qur'an in the grey dawn, and at nights he recited his verses by
lamplight on the steps of the pond, often with Sufia and me as an
audience. His voice was beautiful, and the Arabic verse could be
heard over the whole bari. I suspect I was not quite as respectful as I
should have been, for much as Amma chided me, I could not bring
myself to call this boy by the honorific 'you', '*apni*', and I often
unconsciously committed small but significant sins. 'Eh, Elder Sister,'
he often had to remind me, as I lay stretched out in the moonlight
on the stone seats at the ghat, 'don't put your feet up like that – can't
you see that they're on the same level as our holy Qur'an?'

Then one day, quite inexplicably, Abdul Hossain found that try as hard
as he might, he simply could not remember a word of the Qur'anic

verse which he had now spent three years at the madrasa learning. Until then, his studies had been going well. He had a reputation amongst the other students for great studiousness; he could recite long passages from memory and sang out the Arabic so clearly and tunefully that it was often he who was asked to recite the verses during religious functions or special prayers. He had studied before in Sylhet Town, and it was well known that as long as his father did not need him in his shop, and he passed his exams, he would become a mullah. His elder brothers had all gone to the government school and his father often reminded him that he was honoured to be getting a madrasa education, and that he had great hopes for his son's future.

So Abdul worked hard. At dawn, as the first yellow and silver lights were spreading across the sky, he would pray, and then open up his Qur'an on its special stand and start his reading; to pass his exams he would have to know vast tracts of verse by heart. Then, when the sun had already risen high in the sky and was shining down clear and strong, Amma brought him a great steaming bowl of rice and curry, and he would wrap the Qur'an back into its special cloth, put on his cleanest prayer cap, and set out across the fields for the madrasa, where every day except Friday the wail of students reciting their verses could be heard coming from the small stone building, rising and falling and ringing out over the village until the afternoon call to prayer. In the afternoon Abdul Hossain continued his studies back in the cool dark room which he shared with the goats and ducks. And so on, until late into the night. He often recited his verses until well after everyone else had bolted the doors and gone to bed.

It was the beginning of April and in a few weeks, with the onset of Ramadan, the madrasa would close for the month and the students would return home to swot for their exams, which were held in the town in the middle of the month of fasting. Ahead of them all lay a mammoth test of endurance. No one admitted to dread at the prospect of the time ahead; they all said that Allah would send them strength, and that it would be His wish whether they passed or failed; that with their faith the fasting would not be a problem. Abdul worked particularly hard. He stopped playing marbles in the afternoons with the little boys of the bari, or going out with them to shoot herons with their catapults; he stopped fooling around with the girls in the evening as they gave him his rice, too. Instead, he shut himself into his room, for long, long hours at a stretch and concentrated upon his Qur'an until the Arabic blurred before him.

And then, that morning, he found that he simply could not remember a thing. He thought he had a fever, but decided to go to the madrasa as usual. And there it was even worse. He stared at the script, but it was quite meaningless, just a series of strange scribbles. He tried to chant some verses, but they had slipped completely away from his memory. His head was spinning and he felt sick, he couldn't breathe. He sat motionless in front of his Qur'an until he could bear it no longer. Suddenly, and to the amazement of the other boys, he fell to the ground with a thud.

When they eventually managed to rouse him, he was quite changed. His eyes were open, but he could not utter a word, only the occasional grunt or moan. They shook him and shouted his name, but he did not respond. He sat motionless on the floor while they surrounded him in a frightened crowd. It was certainly a bhut, they all realised that. They stood discussing what they should do while one of them ran to fetch the mullah, who arrived quickly with several of the village elders who had already heard of what had happened.

'It's most likely a *jinni*,' he declared.

According to people in Talukpur there are two sorts of jinn, special Muslim spirits. One is evil and attacks the unprotected for the sheer fun of it; the other is holy and virtuous. These jinn are pious in the extreme. They live in or around mosques and are rumoured to look just like mullahs, with long beards, robes and prayer caps – not, of course, that anyone can see them. They pray, and do the work of Allah; if a mullah has particular power, they may come to him and help him in his work, healing and fighting the evil forces in the world.

'I shall need chillis, some rope, and a stick,' the mullah continued. 'You, Boy, run and get them from the schoolteacher's bari – quickly!'

He was a man who inspired great confidence. His beard was white and bushy and his eyes were calm. He never wasted words but would smile quietly instead of speaking. When necessary, if there was great sickness, he would pray all night over a rigged-up public-address system run from a car battery, which broadcast his words all over the village. By dawn, his voice cracked with emotion and was heavy with tears. He was without doubt the most revered person in Talukpur: women pulled their saris over their heads and turned their faces away from him as he approached, and would never treat him with the easy informality they enjoyed with their village neighbours and kin. Whenever he visited a family, the utmost effort was made to produce for him delicacies of the greatest luxury and expense.

The crowd stood in a hushed group around Abdul Hossain, no one quite sure what to do. One of his friends had returned with a big pot of water and made a great show of splashing it on to the boy's face, but it had no effect. He twitched slightly, but his eyes did not open. At last the child who had been sent off reappeared. He came pushing his way through the huge group of people who now filled the madrasa, brandishing what he had fetched proudly and struggling slightly with the weight of the giant batten he had brought. The mullah said nothing but took the things silently from the little boy's hands.

'Now tie Abdul Hossain up,' he ordered.

They tied his feet together and his hands behind his back. Then they pushed him down on to his knees, where he stayed with his head down, moaning slightly. The mullah leant over him and pushed the fat green chillis he held in his hand up the boy's nostrils. He spluttered slightly, but did not move. Then the mullah gently muttered some words of Arabic and blew on him, to sweep the affliction away with his breaths. Nothing happened. Straightening up, the mullah spoke the powerful holy words more loudly, chanting them with the accustomed ease and strength of a man who gained his living through his holiness.

Then, taking the batten and swinging it over Abdul Hossain's head, he brought it down with a crack across his back. 'Who are you? Why have you come? Why have you captured this boy, Abdul Hossain?' he cried.

The crowd pressed closer, straining every nerve to see and hear what was going on. Some children ran outside to fetch their friends, but the minor commotion they caused was ignored.

'Why have you come?' the mullah shouted again, and once more brought down the batten, this time across Abdul Hossain's chest. He stopped and again began to recite Arabic, but as he whispered the foreign words the boy suddenly jerked, and the chillis flew out of his nostrils.

'I am a jinni! I am a jinni!' he cried.

The mullah hit him, hard this time, and Abdul Hossain fell on to his face. His voice was strangely deep and disjointed.

'Why did you come, bad one?'

'I am a jinni, Master, but I promise I shan't come back! You are the Master!'

Then he sat up again, and began to groan and mutter words which nobody watching could possibly understand. They gripped each other in fear, and recited the names of Allah and Mohammed under their breath, whilst the mullah brandished his stick over the boy and shouted.

'He says he is a holy one!' he announced to the crowd. 'Says this Abdul Hossain insulted him and that is why he has come! ... ' He stopped, and appeared to be listening intently to the jumbled words which spilled out of Abdul Hossain's mouth.

'It was last week, on Friday – this boy, he trod on the jinni-sahib whilst he was praying in the mosque. He did not know that he had done it, but he trod on his toes, and so the jinni-sahib has returned to cause this suffering ... '

'Master-Sahib, I shall never return! Forgive me!' the jinni cried from the boy's mouth. The people standing nearest repeated the speech to those at the back, and a ripple of horror and amazement passed through the crowd.

'I am leaving, Master-Sahib! Don't beat me any more!'

The mullah did not reply but stood back, his batten this time still in his hands. 'He has been punished enough,' he said. 'This time he will not return.'

Abdul Hossain fell back and opened his eyes. Something in their bewildered surprise showed that the jinn had indeed gone. His friends rushed to him with fans and water. They lifted him under the arms and helped him outside. His body ached from the beating, and he had the smell of chillis in his nose; his head was pounding and his throat was hoarse from shouting, but his mind was clear again. He said the name of the Prophet Mohammed and closed his eyes. He was cured.

A month later Abdul Hossain came into the bari yard, flushed and victorious. He had come top in his exams.

'Not many people have special powers like me,' he told me later. 'I can talk with jinn, after all.'

And then, placing his new white prayer cap on his head and smoothing down the silk punjabi he had bought just the week before in Sylhet, he ran into the sunlit yard and out towards the madrasa, where his friends were waiting for him.

8   STORMS

'Come in quickly! Get those pots in from the yard – hurry!'

Amma stood on the verandah, and pulled the thin cotton of her sari closer around her body.

A storm was coming. From gentle blue the sky had turned a vivid purple and the village was rapidly cast into a premature night-time gloom, now lit only by sporadic flashes of white electricity. Clothes on the washing line hanging above the yard swung about frantically, some dropping to the dusty ground, and the wooden shutters on the windows crashed angrily on their hinges, caught innocently unfastened by the sudden and violent wind. The betel trees out by the pond, bent in half by the force of the gale, lashed back and forth until it seemed they must break. Outside, across the land that surrounded the bari, men came running back from the fields where they had been grazing their cattle, holding the giant leaves of banana trees over their heads in anticipation of the downpour and followed by their small gaggles of bulls, trotting back towards cover as anxiously as the humans.

In the yard, everyone rushed frantically to bring in the things which only half an hour ago had been drying in the sun. The children, whipped into a frenzy of excitement, jumped up and down in the darkness and ran from one end of the yard to the other screaming, 'Rain, rain, rain! A storm's coming! A storm's coming!' until their leaps and chanting turned into a veritable rain dance and they eventually collapsed, exhausted and laughing, as the wind swept over them.

It had certainly been dry for months now, and this storm was long overdue. It was to be the first of many, heralding the beginning of the monsoon. They were ferocious affairs, which silenced the birds and drove everyone inside to huddle under their roofs and watch the driving rain outside. For those like us, with concrete or tin covering the bari buildings, shelter was more or less assured. For the others, with straw roofs and walls of mud and bamboo, the storms could mean disaster, and literally a broken home. Sometimes there was hail, great lumps of it as big as marbles, and always the horizon flashed with sheets of lightning and the village shook with the force of the thunder.

'It's going to rain,' Amma announced wisely to me.

'Is that good?'

'Of course! How will our paddy grow without rain? Allah's sent this for us.'

As she spoke, the rain started. It came slowly at first and then, gathering confidence, began to pour down on to the yard, turning everything into a grey blur. We stood and watched from the verandah, mesmerised by the power of the storm. The children were quiet now and squatted together on the steps, shivering in the unaccustomed cold. It seemed almost impossible that anything left outside could survive the force of the downpour.

'Who's that?' Amma pulled her sari quickly over her head and peered out into the deluge.

'What?'

'There's someone coming ... Yshh! It's Hassan Ali.'

She was right. Coming out of the haze of wind and water was a man. He was the servant of Kudi Bibi's bari; he helped her now aged brothers to farm their land, and ensured the smooth running of the homestead. He had been living in the village for many years now, and everyone in the family called him 'Mama' (maternal uncle). His fictive role meant that like other long-term labourers he was treated with easy familiarity; he was like a poor and inferior relative, for whom appearances did not have to be kept up. Indeed, rather than his presence threatening the modesty of household women, he was welcomed by them, and given betel nut and pan to chew on his visits. He was, after all, an important source of village gossip for them. Now, he was running with sure feet across the rivulets of sand and water which the yard had become, although it was already treacherously slippery.

'Khala!' ('Aunt!') he cried as soon as he was close enough for Amma to hear him through the beating rain. 'Where's Sassa?' (He meant Abba.) 'Fetch him quickly – a thief has come to our bari, and my master's out visiting the village of his father-in-law!'

'Ya Allah!' Amma jumped up and ran inside to wake Abba. He always retreated to bed in wet weather, for it gave him rheumatism and made his joints throb with pain.

'What happened, Mama?' The children, agog with curiosity, surrounded Hassan Ali, who stood impatiently in the dry, dripping on to the earth floor.

'Did you see him?'

'Was he big? Was he black? Can we come and catch him too?'

'It's not for babies, Little Brother!' Najma, who had been watching from the doorway, cuffed the impertinent Saller – who was, after all, only six – round the head, and he went off howling inside.

'You can fetch a stick,' Hassan Ali told Mobed, and the boy went off proudly to bring the huge cane which Abba kept behind the door for beating robbers. In a few years' time he would be old enough to wield it himself.

The teenage cousins from next door had also come rushing out on hearing the news of a thief, with more sticks, and chains, which I had previously noticed hanging on the wall but for some reason had never enquired about. Eventually Abba too appeared, his face set in grim determination and his air rifle under his arm. Many of the richer families had guns.

The men all set off together, splashing purposefully across the yard to the bari next door. The rain had subsided slightly now, and the birds had once more begun to sing.

By dusk the clouds had swept back, revealing an undisturbed sky beneath. A few remained, but were reduced from their looming darkness to a pink fluffiness which skimmed the horizon and were reflected in the fresh puddles which lay everywhere. Abba and the young men had resumed to the bari several hours earlier.

'He got away,' Abba declared, throwing himself on to his bed and groaning in misery from his aching body.

'Did you see him, Abazie?' Mobed climbed up beside his father and began to massage his feet and legs, as he knew he liked when his pains were plaguing him.

'There was nothing to see! That old thief came creeping in and took a cow from my cousin's sheds before anyone knew what had happened. Then Hassan Ali saw the doors were open and only one of the beasts was left.'

'Is my cousin back yet, has he heard?' Amma asked, setting her husband's hookah down in front of him.

'He's heard. He's so hot with anger that his wife will have to fan him for hours to make his head cool again. He says he'll give one hundred taka to the man that brings the thief to him, and then he'll beat him senseless. The wife of young Abus Meer says she saw a strange man, but was too busy getting things in from the rain to tell anyone.'

'That girl's a fool,' Amma muttered.

'Can't you call the police?' I put in.

'Pah! What can they do? Our Bangladeshi police are miles away. No, if we catch him then we might hand him over if we choose, but they won't do anything now.'

It was certainly true that the police force counted for little outside the nearest town, and the villagers usually had to solve crimes and mete out punishment as they thought fit, quite autonomously. Indeed, if a bari had no able men living on it, there was little to stop the bandits of whom everyone spoke with such fear storming in, bashing down the doors, and making off with whatever they chose. A decade earlier, during the years of constant political disruption, coups and famine in Bangladesh, I was told that this was relatively common, and the village people had not yet forgotten the violent bands which had terrorised the country in those days of mayhem and lawlessness.

'Will you really beat the thief if he is caught, Abba?' I asked, horrified at the thought of this gentle man being involved in such an act. I still found it hard to reconcile religiosity with the uncompromising and unflinching acceptance of violence amongst most people in the village.

'Of course, Beti! Don't you punish criminals in London? If a man steals, then we beat him, in the name of Allah. It's our duty. Child, rub my back now.'

The thief was caught the next day, during the clear blue morning, which showed no trace of the storm the day before. They fetched him from the bazaar, where he had been found, and brought him to Kudi Bibi's bari, where he was to be tried. A great gaggle of excited men and boys pushed the chained man along in front of them as they approached the bari, taking the occasional swipe at him as they went.

Everyone in the village knew what had happened, and that the man who was now passing their baris in such a dejected manner was the thief who had stolen a bull from Kudi Bibi's bari. The women ran out into their yards when they saw the small procession approaching, peering round the banana-leaf fences which encircled their yards and sending their children down the paths to follow the men and report back on what they had seen.

'Did you see the thief?' everyone asked one another all day. 'Was he evil-looking? – Did you see him being beaten? – Who beat him hardest?'

In our own bari, the women had been gathered in the undergrowth on the homestead edges in anticipation of the excitement ever since Banessa had appeared with the news that she had heard that the man had been caught in the bazaar, eating *ruti* (unleavened bread) at a tea-stall. They knew that he would be brought back to face the aggrieved brother of Kudi Bibi, and were anxious to get a look at him. Abba had already left for his cousin's bari. It was important that he, as one of the elder members of the lineage, should be involved in the decision of what to do with the man.

Across the fields which separated the two baris we could see that many of the village men had already gathered in Kudi Bibi's yard. Some of the most respected elders, such as Saiyed Ali, who had hobbled over to his neighbour's homestead as soon as he heard what had happened, had been given chairs to sit on and were now installed under the shade of one of the giant 'Flame of the Forest' trees which had recently exploded into startlingly orange flowers, and were now scattered across the green and brown countryside like beacons in the otherwise uniform landscape. Saiyed Ali had been to many such meetings before. He had been one of the most influential men on the panchayat since before the British left Bengal, and even now he never missed a chance to demonstrate to the younger men the extent of his knowledge. But still, these days he was also forced to admit that his hearing was a little less sharp, and yes, he had once or twice – he was sure it was no more – nodded off in the middle of a particularly involved discussion on land rights. The young men of the village meanwhile milled around the yard, gossiping and swapping news. Someone from nearly every well-connected family was there. Crime was a community affair, and the villagers knew how to deal with it.

Then there was a commotion amongst the waiting men, and we could see from the knot of figures coming into the centre of the yard that the thief and his captors had arrived.

'Can you see? I can't make a thing out with these eyes of mine,'
Amma was saying.

'Are you going to go over and see?' Najma asked me.

'I don't know. Would they mind?' These days, I found entering
the world of the village men more and more difficult. It was not that
they were unfriendly, but simply that I did not, and never would, belong
with them.

'No ... You should go and see it all.'

'Are you coming?'

'Yshh, there are so many men there! Anyway, I can't be bothered
today. You can go with Banessa. She's going.'

And so Banessa and I went off together to see what was to happen
to the thief. It was strange, I thought as we walked out towards the
great group of men in the next-door bari; in some ways we were both
outsiders, who therefore stood beyond the rules applying to most village
women: Banessa because of her poverty, and I because of my huge
wealth and privilege.

Kudi Bibi smiled and took my hand when she saw me. She was
busy boiling up a huge pot of tea at the back of the homestead, away
from the numerous male eyes.

'Yah Allah! Have you just walked through that great crowd of men?
Ma! Didn't you cover your head from them?'

She pushed a basket of rice at Banessa and motioned her to go down
to the pond to wash it, then pulled the pot off the fire and set it on
the floor, wiping her hands on her sari.

'Have you see the thief?'

'Not yet.'

'I'll take you to look at him.'

'Where is he?'

'In that room at the end of the bari. They put him in there the minute
he arrived. They're deciding what to do with him now.'

'How do they know he took the bull?'

'The man was stupid – a fool! He went off over the fields, in front
of whole villages with our animal, so people saw him. Then word got
to us that he'd been seen, and we heard from someone else that his
name was Abdul Ali from Kande village. Our Hassan Ali went to his
bari last night, and there was the bull he'd been looking after since it
was a calf. But the beta had run off. So what could everyone do but

wait until the morning, then go off looking for him? They found him in the bazaar, thanks be to God.'

'What will they do to him?'

'Beat him, Beti. Then take him to the police, or maybe let him go. They say he was once richer than he is now, and his brother still has some land, so perhaps if he sells that he can pay our panchayat a fine. I don't know. It's men's work.'

'Will the panchayat give him a trial?'

Kudi Bibi was prising open a huge tin of sugar, and adding it to the tea. She was not rich, and I knew that she could barely afford the sugar, but it was a special occasion and she must do her duty and feed the honoured visitors well. She was always generous, despite her money problems; whenever I visited, she insisted on sending a child to the bazaar for biscuits.

'You must ask the men if you want to know things like that. That's not for me to say. Hey, Bebi!' She beckoned one of her brother's daughters. 'Take Katy to look at the thief.'

The little girl took my hand and led me out through the building, into the bright sunshine. The men were still standing around looking purposeful, but doing nothing. We slipped through the crowd, Bebi giggling when I exchanged greetings with the men, and came to the bangla-ghor on the other side of the yard.

'Look!' she told me, and pushed me towards the building. Its doors were not only closed, but chained and fastened with an imposing lock. A small group of boys were already peering through the gaps in the bamboo wall, but made way to give me a look.

'Come and see!' they cried at me. 'He's really ugly!'

Feeling slightly queasy, I peered through the wall. Inside the room, in the middle of the dirt floor, with heavy chains around his almost naked body, was an old man. He was sitting crosslegged, with his head down and his face turned away from me. His shoulders were slumped under the chains, and his hands were folded in his lap, in total surrender. He was very, very dirty, and his lungi was torn. I suppose he was about sixty, although like so many of the village people, with the weight of his life about him, he looked many years older.

'Can you see?' Bebi asked me.

'Yes.'

'If you wait, then you'll be able to see my cousins beating him.'

'No, I don't feel well, I'm going back to my bari. I don't like to
see things like that. I don't think it's good.'

Bebi fixed me with her large brown eyes. She was eleven, and very
bright. 'Didn't he steal a bull? Don't you know how much a bull costs?
How can Abba plough his land without his bulls? You can't have robbers
stealing people's cows. This man deserves a beating. That's our way
of punishment.'

A few hours later the men pulled the thief out into the yard, and
beat him with a large wooden batten. A huge crowd had gathered
to see, but from our bari the women could glimpse only the great
jostling group of men, and hear their shouts. I did not go to watch,
but saw instead the young cousins coming home much later, their
faces flushed with the exertion of having given the man a beating.
It had been their duty as the young of the lineage and they seemed
to have enjoyed it. The elders had watched with approval and only
a very few, who had been educated, outside the village, had shaken
their heads in disapproval.

Later, the thief's brother came to talk to some of the older men in
the village. (The bull had been returned earlier in the day.) He was
younger, but carried with him the same air of resignation as his
brother. He had put on his only shirt to make the visit, and it was
crumpled and tight under his arms. He talked with the elders for many
hours, and eventually they agreed not to hand their captive over to
the town police. That would have meant another beating, perhaps,
and many thousands of taka in bribes to get him released. The village
panchayat, it seemed, had been merciful. Many hours after the moon
had appeared over the trees, the huge red globe turning silver as it
rose in the sky, the thief was released. He walked out of the village
by the main path beside his brother, a small hunched man with the
marks of his beating slashed across his shoulders and back. No one came
to stare this time, for it was too late, and most of the villagers were
sleeping. But still, the brothers were afraid of meeting any of the locals,
and hurried past the baris as fast as they could.

By the time the path had taken them out of Talukpur and into the
next village, the moon had disappeared under sudden clouds, and forks
of lightning across the sky threw their faces into fleeting brightness.
They knew then that there would soon be another storm, and unless
they hurried even faster they would be caught out in the violent rain.

9   ABDULLAH SEEKS A CURE

By August the pattern of sudden storms which came from nowhere and ended quickly, had given way to the monsoon proper. I lay on my bed listening to the steady drip of water coming in through the rough plaster ceiling to muddy my floor and dampen my saris; it was 5 a.m., as chilly as winter, and once again it was raining. Abba had already said his prayers, but now he was snoring again, and like him everyone else lay huddled under the covers, shivering and predicting fever. The bari was completely still, and strangely quiet. The little boys who usually filled it with noise had gone out fishing, running splashing through the yard before dawn with their spears and pots from the kitchen. When they returned them later in the day, they would be filled with fish from the waterlogged fields. Rain, rain, rain. The days of early rising to wash in the cool morning sunlight seemed distant now, and even the birds, which in other seasons greeted the day uproariously, appeared to prefer the silence of sleep.

The monsoon had continued for at least a month, and once more the village was transformed. The paths had disintegrated into impassable mud, and the river was full again. These days, to get anywhere I had to call one of the bari labourers to take me across the water and then, umbrella in hand, clamber aboard the bari's rickety old boat, usually accompanied by a gaggle of goats being taken to the other side of the river for grazing.

The rains meant that the small activities around which I hung my days had suddenly become difficult and exhausting. The bari yard, usually sandy earth, had changed into a treacherous pit of the most slippery mud imaginable. Every day I managed to lose a flip-flop in it, and every day I escaped landing on my bottom by the merest fraction. To get to the pond to bathe became quite a challenge, and I usually came back muddier than before my wash. Trips to the latrine were equally nerve-racking. If it was actually raining – and it usually was – I set off with my water-pot, my umbrella and, at night, my lantern, to slide through the muddy morass which had once been our bari until, exhausted and victorious, I reached my destination. For the first time I cursed my sari for the way it trailed in the mud, and fantasised about clean, indoor, dry Western lavatories. The word 'bog' began to have special meanings for me, and every day I prayed fervently that now would not be the time when dysentery struck. Infuriatingly, everyone else walked with sure and confident feet through the mud, and never slipped. Even more mystifyingly, if I was wading through deep swampiness I always arrived on the other side having been joined by several plump black leeches hanging on to my feet and ankles, yet whilst my companions screamed '*Jook! Jook!*' and scurried around me to pick them off, their own limbs were invariably free of the dreaded creatures.

During the worst of the rains, life in the village seemed to slow down until it came almost to a standstill. There was little work for the labourers except cutting back the frantically growing water hyacinth, which was fed to the cattle, and fishing out in the flooded fields, and many men complained bitterly that over these months obtaining money for food was a struggle which often ended in hunger and indebtedness. Social calls, as well as work, also stopped. People could move around only by boat now, for most of the village tracks were covered in water, and the rickshaws and motorbikes that had been a common sight a few months earlier had completely disappeared. But although most people preferred to stay within the confines of their baris, for others trips outside were unavoidable, and the wooden boats which all through the dry season had lain discarded in the water lilies were again put to work. Every morning, too, the 'engine boat' would come down the river, piled high with village men in their best lungis and umbrellas out on a trip to Sylhet or Nobiganj (the nearest town). These days, instead of recognising figures over the fields, we would spot bamboo boats with painted cabins or great cloth sails slowly moving through the water lilies.

A few hours later, when the rain had subsided a little, Amma came into my room and handed me a cup of hot, sweet tea, and some fried cakes which she had prepared specially for me.

'Are you going over to the bari of your brother, Abdullah?' she asked.
'Why?'

'He's sick, and their house is flooded. The *kobiraj* will be coming.
If you go, they'll all be pleased.'

Abdullah's bari lay on the edge of the village out in fields owned
by his prosperous cousin. He had once had his own land, but he had
never managed to make a profit from it. As his family grew and grew
and he found himself with nine children to feed, he had to take loans
to pay for the extra rice and food. The interest rates were so high that
soon the only way he could satisfy the moneylender was by giving his
fields as security. Within a year, they were all gone. Abdullah had put
his thumbprint on the forms the moneylender had pushed in front of
him, and he was landless. It happened to many households without
enough land to supply their everyday needs, who fell into the slippery
pit of interest-loaded loans. Now he and his family lived as best they
could in the tiny shack which they shared with a couple of goats and
hens, and a large number of cockroaches. There were eight of them,
not including the daughters who had married into different villages.
His brother's widow, with her clan of children, lived next door. She
was totally destitute now, without her husband's wages, and survived
by begging from her richer relatives or labouring for a handful of rice
a day.

Today, the yard outside the huts was filled with water, and inside
it was creeping several inches up the dried-mud walls, which were
sagging sadly in the kitchen. The family bed had been raised on stilts,
and a small heap of possessions was balanced on a bar supporting the
ceiling. If the water level rose further they would have to abandon
their home and disperse to the baris of relatives in drier locations. They
prayed to Allah that this would not happen.

'You've come!'

Rushida, the middle daughter, grabbed my wrist and touched my
nose roughly with hers, the village gesture of affection.

'Abazie is very ill. Come and look at him.'

Abdullah lay on the bed covered by a thin blanket, groaning as his
youngest daughters massaged his legs and sprinkled water over his head.
The sharp outline of his bony body was painfully clear through the
material. From time to time he closed his eyes and murmured to himself,
then moaned again. He had been like this for three days now, and the
family were frightened. Three days in which he had not been able to

work in the fields had meant three days without the precious wages which helped them to struggle on. No money meant no food bought from the bazaar, no nothing.

'Ya Allah, what troubles we have! No one can have problems like ours!' Rushida was sighing. 'First we're sent this water, and then Abba is so sick his brain is hardly here at all. Can't you give us some money for medicines?'

I was one of many being asked to help the family. Already that morning Abdullah's wife, Matoc Bibi, had taken her patched and battered umbrella and gone to visit relatives with requests for money. They would not starve in the near future, of that they could be sure, but this sickness could put the labourer out of action for weeks, maybe months. Already they did not have enough money to buy cooking oil and chillis) in the bazaar, and their small stock of rice was running worryingly low. Abdullah might even die. After all, for a poor man who had lived long enough to father nine children and see the eldest married, death was not so unusual.

He had been bothered by his cough for many months now. No one could remember when it had first begun, but recently it had certainly been getting worse, especially in the wet weather, and now here he was with a head as hot as boiling rice, and so weak that he could hardly walk without help. Early that morning his eldest daughter had arrived from her husband's village, having heard the news that her father was ill. She stood over him now and stroked his head as she cried quietly to herself. She had always cared more for her father than anyone, and before she was married she would spend hours rubbing his back for him when he came home exhausted from the fields.

Other visitors had come, too, to see the sick man. Like Abdullah they were all labourers, and squatted on the dry parts of the floor smoking bedis and talking about village politics and the general lack of work which always descended with the rains. Abdullah was too ill to join in, and he ignored them as they argued over the council elections and told the story of how a man in another village had burnt down his enemy's house in a dispute over land. The eldest and most respected among them was angrily declaring that this was the fate of anyone who tried to go against Mustaf Ali.

'Why did he do such things?' he was saying. 'The man is a fool. Everyone knows that he who fights with big men such as that Mustaf *dada* [senior man] will be broken. It is his fault, and now he is crying that his family have nowhere to sleep. Well, he should have thought of that before ... '

'Ai! If Allah wills it, we'll all be beggars within a year. The world is full of cheats.'

The other men nodded in agreement and looked over to Abdullah, who was now sleeping. It was not usually talked of, but everyone knew how he had lost land. Although they were all sometimes forced to take loans from moneylenders, it was generally agreed that they were cheating sinners; it was written in the Qur'an, after all, that interest should never be charged.

'Oh, Brother, are you sleeping?' they said to him. 'The healing man will be here soon, Allah willing. Hey! Come, Little Sister, and bring us some more betel nut!'

The healer who had been summoned to cure Abdullah was a distant relative, like most of the people in the village. He had spent three years in the madrasa when he was a boy, and this had earned him the privilege of being called 'Mullah' by those who had faith in him, a title of considerable prestige. His days in the bare stone building under the strict supervision of the village Imam meant that he now knew enough to write the powerful Arabic words on fragments of paper and make them into *tabij* (amulets). He could also 'give *foo*', a skill which involved blowing away the afflictions of the sick. Only the madrasa-educated religious elite could ever do this.

The healer made his living by such services. He carried a pile of battered books and papers telling him which words should be written for each type of sickness, and what should be whispered – the holy spells – with the giving of foo. Many villagers were disdainful of him, and preferred the government doctor at the bazaar to traditional healers of such meagre repute. Others, however, trusted him implicitly: without the protection and power of Allah's words, how would they ever get well? And so he had enough patients to keep him busy, and was often to be seen walking into the village on the paths and across the fields, with his book under his arm and his prayer cap gleaming in the sunshine.

Now it was the turn of Abdullah's family to wait for the healer to arrive. He had promised he would come early in the morning, having been sent for the night before, but already we could hear the distant sounds of the midday call to prayer.

'Do you think he'll come?' I whispered to Rushida as we chewed betel together at the back of the hut. I was anxious to see more of his work.

'Who knows? Allah only knows. People like mullahs don't pay much attention to us poor.'

But suddenly Abdullah's youngest son came running in and announced that he had seen the mullah's boat slowly approaching across the flooded land.

The daughters of the family pulled their saris over their heads and tried to blend into the rough mud walls when the mullah entered the hut. Since Abdullah's bari comprised only one room, there was nowhere else for them to go. The kitchen was a small open mud fireplace protected by a bamboo roof and banana leaves, but this had been partially destroyed by the rains. They had their large wooden bed which people used for sitting on during the day, some mats for other members of the family to lie on, and a collection of pillows and rags on which to make themselves comfortable. Someone had attempted to paper over the cracks in the walls with sheets from an old school book gleaned from richer relatives. Guests who could understand written English, of which there were very few, could therefore broaden their minds by examining the walls and reading: 'How beautifully the stars peep and reflect on the ponds, rivers, seas and lakes. And when it lets loose its rapid turning wind the cloud makes a bridge of it from cape to cape.' And further on, covered in scribbles made from some overzealous student, 'It is not pelt and power or high titles that make a man immortal. It is the patriotic zeal in a man which brings undying glory for a man.' I had never been able to explain to Abdullah's family why their wallpaper made me laugh so.

But the mullah did not have time for such musings. He bustled into the room with a hurried greeting of 'Salaam-e-lekum', and made straight for the patient. He did not like visiting such poor families, but it had to be admitted that the rich and prestigious villagers rarely enlisted his skills. He was a small, flabby little man with pebble glasses, a ragged beard, and a frayed punjabi shirt which was distinctly grubby. He stood over Abdullah and put a hand on his forehead.

'Yes, yes,' he was muttering, 'oh yes, how many times does Allah not send this sickness to us?'

He sat down on the bed and began to spread out his books with a flourish. 'Bring me string, Little Son, and paper and a pen.'

This caused a minor panic. They had once had a pen but it had ended up with the scattered remnants of broken flip-flops, bones, and cracked water-pots outside. The child was sent to the family of a neighbouring bari who had a son at school, and after a few minutes he returned triumphantly. The kobiraj wrote a few words of Arabic on the paper, rolled it into a small ball, tied it with cotton, and then slipped it into a tiny metal casket to be hung round Abdullah's neck on a piece of string. The strength of these words would release him from his illness. Then he leant over him and, closing his eyes, whispered the secret holy words of healing. He took Abdullah's head into his hands and blew hard on to it three times.

'There,' he said. 'It is finished.'

He was tactfully slipped a ten-taka note and then, gathering up the tools of his craft, he swiftly left for more fruitful sickbeds.

The family had also decided that Abdullah should be given medicine, and it was for this that they had asked me for money. What they wanted more than anything was to give him an injection. Many people in the village believed that injections cured everything and restored strength. Everyone who could afford it had them, and they were prescribed by the government doctor for almost every illness. No one knew what they were, or how they worked, but that was not the point. They were from the town, and were associated with the ways of a modern, developed world. They had power, and so the villagers put their faith in them.

But an injection would cost over one hundred taka, and no one knew how they would ever be able to raise so much. Abdullah's eldest son worked as a cow herder for one of the biggest landowners in the village, but he was still a boy and his wages hardly kept the family supplied with a week's spices, let alone the luxury of special drugs. Then there were all the other medicines, the capsules and syrups which came from the bazaar. The doctor, whom Abdullah's son had visited, had listened to the list of ailments and hastily and unintelligibly written out a prescription. It included five drugs, and their total price had come to over two hundred taka, far more than a week's wages. The boy could not understand the instructions, but the man in the dispensary had told him that they would have to repeat the prescription the next week for it to be effective. So he had bought only the first two medicines on the list, and now a bottle of cough mixture, a year past its expiry date, and a packet of aspirin were standing on the dirt floor of the hut.

Matoc Bibi did not return until after sunset, and I met her on the river-bank as I myself returned home. She had been walking quickly, in fear of the approaching darkness and its bhut, and was out of breath, but as always she had enough energy to grab my arm and insist I pay another visit to Abdullah.

'You may have already visited, but I wasn't there then, was I? You must see my husband again, otherwise I'll be angry!' she cried as she pulled me into the hut.

Inside, the family quickly gathered around her and watched expectantly as she put down her umbrella and squatted on her heels. She had once been pretty, but years of childbirth and bitter poverty had totally erased any lingering traces of her youthful looks. Her teeth were rotten from insufficient food and reddened from pan-chewing, her greying hair was thin and brittle, and her body was so skinny that her breasts had almost totally disappeared and her legs stuck out from her worn sari like twigs. But still, like so many of the village women, she had a kind of beauty, and her face usually beamed with smiles. Everyone liked Matoc Bibi.

She loosened a small bundle tied into her sari and took out a handful of chillis and the couple of betel nuts which her relatives had donated.

'What happened?' her daughter asked.

'Oh Daughter, what suffering there has been today! Your uncle has gone to Sylhet and all the bari were out visiting with only that little cousin of yours alone grinding spices, just like a servant girl. So I asked her, when do they come? Before midday prayer, she says. So I wait. They don't come. So I wait, and they don't come until after the afternoon prayer. That aunt of yours was wearing yet another new sari! Four hundred taka, she said. Oh, what beauty! But she still refused to give me that old green one. What sort of wife my cousin has, I can't say. Oh Golden Mother, Oh Daughter, no one knows why Allah has given me such a fate as this. Here's your *babazie* sick, and no rice cooked, and your sickness coming too ... '

And at this point she blew her nose out on to the floor, for she was crying. Her daughter would soon be giving birth to another baby.

'But what did they give?'

'Two hundred. So we can pay for that medicine, and still go to our Pir-Saheb's bari. Oh Allah, I pray to You every day to give us Your help. Has your father's fever lessened?'

'It's the same.'

'We'll catch the engine boat that goes past Fitua; my cousin told me all about it. Then we'll only have to walk a little way to see Pir-Saheb. That'll be five taka each way for the four of us. Your middle brother shall come too, so that's forty taka. Then we can still afford to buy a chicken and offer it to Pir-Saheb.'

She spat a stream of red spittle from her pan on to the floor.

'But Mother, Babazie is too ill to go so far.'

Matoc Bibi was a very religious woman and set great store by the healing power of the saint's burial place. 'He can lie in the boat, can't he? We'll go on Friday, that'll be a good day for it. Will you come too, Elder Sister?'

I said that of course I would join them. A visit to their saint's shrine would be a real treat for me.

'Come, girl, aren't you going to cook any rice?' Matoc Bibi went on after we'd settled that I would go too. 'That cousin of yours gave me nothing, and my belly gives me pain, it's so angry.'

By Friday Abdullah was feeling slightly better, and his head was less hot. He could sit up, and even walk short distances with a stick. It was going to be a fine day, the sky was clear of clouds for once, so it was decided that we would go to see the saint. I arrived as everyone was preparing for the expedition, changing into their best clothes – mostly hand-outs from richer relatives – and oiling their hair with the remnants of a bottle Amma had donated the day before. The youngest son of the family was dressed in shorts and a shirt and stood selfconsciously on the muddy floor, shyly avoiding my eye. Out in the fields with his mates he would often assail me and insist that I visit his bari, but now I was here, and on such an important occasion, he had been struck dumb. The household women had been up late into the night preparing a pot of biriani which was going to be given as an offering at the shrine. Such offerings were always distributed as alms to the destitute who hung around shrines, as an act of worship to please Allah and gain the prayers of the saint, be he dead or living. It had cost them the last of their money, and they had had to kill one of their two hens, but they knew that they had a duty to give as much as possible at the shrine.

Before the sun had risen above the line of trees on the horizon, we were already on our way; the engine boat had been hailed as it made its way up river, the sick man helped on board, seats found for our small group on the wooden boards of the boat, and Talukpur left behind. The endlessly green and waterlogged landscape drifted past. Sometimes we saw huts which had been almost completely submerged by the recent flooding. A line of bricks indicated that a wall lay under the water, or the pathetic top leaves of a banana tree showed that what we were chugging over in the engine boat was actually a piece of homestead land. When the boat reached a village it was invariably stopped by cries, and more people piled on. After an hour or so, there were so many people on board that they all had to sit hunched up, and some men had moved out on to the roof. The women squatted in a tiny area curtained off from the men. I was eyed with curiosity and sometimes amazement by the women who joined the boat at each stop, as I always was when I journeyed out of the village.

'Who's that?' Matoc Bibi and her daughter were constantly asked.

'That's our elder sister. She lives in our village.'

'Does she understand our words?'

'Oh yes.'

'Can she eat rice?'

Here, Matoc Bibi would pull a mournful face and sigh pathetically. Just a tiny amount. And she only eats it once a day ... '

I never failed to be amazed by the way my dietary habits were known by the entire village.

'Does she have parents?' The questions continued, with sure predictability. My genealogical details were explained by Matoc Bibi with far greater accuracy than I could ever achieve. I relished the opportunity of letting someone else speak for me, so as Matoc Bibi enjoyed her sudden celebrity at being seen with me, I sat with downcast eyes, feigning shyness and watching the passing floodlands.

Soon attention wandered from the strange foreign beti with the poor-looking women from Talukpur. The women shared pan and began to ask each other about their families and where they were going.

'My eldest son is in London,' one woman was saying. She was wearing a burqua, and the hem of her sari, which hung down below it, showed that it was made of silk, and very expensive. Matoc Bibi had never owned such a sari as this. The woman had a padded face and pudgy fingers, telling of a life of ease.

'Actually, most of my family are there. Except our youngest son, he's in Dhaka now. A business – he has his own house there, of course. Only last week we gave our daughter in marriage to a family in London. Oh yes, Allah has sent us a good boy for her.' She took a large lump of betel from a plastic pouch, and popped it into her mouth.

Another woman was silent throughout the whole journey. She wore a worn, plain sari and her face was tight with thinness and anxiety. The other women heard her speak only when she started in a desperate, panicky voice to argue with the boatman over how much change he should have given her from her ten taka note. It was obvious that she was travelling alone.

Matoc Bibi told them she was going to Fitua. 'Allah has sent us such troubles,' she said. 'This is my eldest girl. How sick her father is! So we're going to see the shrine of the pir-saheb at Fitua and make him an offering. Such a large pot of chicken we have with us. We'll be eating plain rice for the rest of the month.'

She felt a small rush of pride in telling them this. She may not have fine saris or sons in London, but she knew how to please Allah, and was not stingy in her offerings to him. No one would ever be able to say that. The other women smiled approvingly, and began to talk about their own illnesses.

Neither Matoc Bibi nor her daughter had ever been to Fitua before. Both had been once to Sylhet to see the doctor when the youngest son, who was then only a baby, had been ill, and then to the great shrine and mosque of Shah Jalal, the great saint of Sylhet, to get his blessings, but the Fitua shrine was new to them. They had heard of its power, though. One woman in the village was said to have been cured of her blindness by drinking water from the pond. Everyone had said that this would be one of the best places to take Abdullah.

After two hours, every time the boat stopped, Matoc Bibi asked, 'Where is this? Are we there yet?'

'The next village, Auntie, the next village ... ' the boatman cried.

At last we arrived and clambered out of the boat, wading through thick mud to reach dry land. Like all the villages in the area, the beginnings and endings of Fitua were indistinguishable. It was a series of baris spread out over the paddy fields, most of which had now become green islands of land rising out of the water. In the distance was a mosque with its brightly painted stone fronting. Matoc Bibi looked around her. She did not feel comfortable outside her own village, which she had never left for more than a couple of days on visits. Since Abdullah was her cousin as well as her husband, she had not had to move to a new village on her marriage.

'Where's the shrine, then?' she asked.

We started walking, Abdullah leaning heavily on a stick and moving slowly and painfully. His wife and daughter walked on either side of him. Since they had only one umbrella this was taken by the daughter, for as a young woman her modesty was more at risk. I walked a bit behind, covering my face with my sari as much as I could, for experience had taught me that crowds were apt to gather in strange villages when word got round that a white woman had arrived. The little boy brought up the rear, with the pot of biriani under his arm. He was only eight, and he found it very heavy. Every time they passed someone on the path, Matoc Bibi and her daughter asked where they would find the shrine. Everyone they stopped pointed up the path. 'That way, oh look, just by those trees, not too far,' they were told.

They found it at last on the other side of the village under a cluster of giant trees which towered above them, their huge roots spreading out over the ground like fossilised snakes. The shrine was housed in a building brightly painted in as many colours as possible, with stars and flowers. It was surrounded by a large wall and gate, which closed off other small graves. There was a pond to one side, in which pilgrims could cleanse themselves before paying their respects to the shrine. A small group of men sat talking under the trees. Already one or two children with bowls in their hands had gathered for the distribution of food which would constitute the family's offering to the saint, and to Allah. Word always got round quickly, and within five minutes a huge crowd of beggars would be squatting in the dust waiting for their food.

The mullah who looked after the shrine appeared. He had a bushy white beard and an aged-looking prayer cap. It was by no means one of the most important shrines in the area, and the pickings were not particularly big. Shah Jalal's shrine attracted hundreds every day. He was said by local Muslims to be the founder of Islam in Bengal, whose powers had defeated the evil Hindu king who then ruled over it, and to have brought light to Sylhet, the land of the saints. His shrine was always crowded with pilgrims and beggars who lived on the alms they gave: everybody who could visited the shrine of Shah Jalal. But the one we had come to today was only the burial ground of one of the great saint's disciples, in quite a different category.

Without speaking the mullah led the menfolk to the shrine gates, which he unlocked with a large key. Abdullah's son's eyes widened. He had never been inside such a place before. We stayed outside and peered over the wall at what was going on, forbidden, as usual, to go inside. Matoc Bibi muttered the few words of Arabic which she knew. Her daughter looked at the pretty decorations on the shrine and said a prayer for the child inside her. She was hoping it would be a boy.

After Abdullah had prostrated himself on the floor in front of the shrine, his son carefully copying him, they were led out, walking backwards so as not to show disrespect to the saint. Then they began to dole out portions of food to the beggars. Matoc Bibi knew that if her husband died, if Allah sent great misfortune, there would be little to keep her from becoming one of the skinny women in rags waiting patiently with coconut shells and cracked bowls for alms.

'Give the mullah this,' she whispered to her son, and stuffed a ten-taka note into his hand. That was the end of the two hundred taka. They now had no hope of buying any more medicines.

We reached home just before the sun had disappeared behind the familiar line of thatched roofs and palm trees. Large bats had already started to swoop over the water, and the river path was crowded with boys bringing cattle and goats back from grazing. It had been a long day. Abdullah was sleeping, curled into a ball on the floor of the boat. Matoc Bibi had finished her supply of pan and also had her eyes closed. She was thinking of the saint and the reassuring words of the mullah. He had given them a small bottle of water from the shrine.

'Take this every day,' he had said. 'It will cure any sickness. Make sure he doesn't forget, Sister.'

She held the bottle now, and another filled with holy soil from the site of the shrine. This too had great healing powers, and if they rubbed it on Abdullah's chest his cough would go. Things would be all right. He would be cured. Now she could see their own bari – two mud huts, her green sari draped over a bush to dry, the white spots of the pot she hung over her tiny vegetable plot to deter the evil eye, and one of her daughters crouching in the yard picking through the *dhal* for the evening meal. It had not rained for over twenty-four hours now, and the day's heat had rapidly dried away most of the water, leaving large patches of the bari yard only slightly muddy. It seemed as if for now, at least, the flood was over. There would in fact be many more weeks of heavy rain and the destruction which it brought, but for now the world seemed better than it had in the morning.

'Come on, Girl,' she said to her eldest daughter, 'our bari has come. Are you coming to visit us now, Elder Sister? We can get word back to your father's bari that you're here, and he'll send a boat ... '

Matoc Bibi gave me a toothless grin. She was pleased that she was once more in her own village. It had been an important day's work, and she had enjoyed seeing all the other places and talking with the women on the boat, but it was always good to return home. After all, she had work to get on with, for now here it was, nearly sunset, and if she did not hurry with her cooking the family's meal of rice would be late.

10   ALIM ULLAH GOES TO SAUDI

'Hey, Sister!'

I stuck my nose in the air, and ignored the young man gesturing at me from the other side of the road. After three weeks in Talukpur I was on my way to Dhaka, a break I had been looking forward to for the whole of the preceding week. I had left the village at sunset to give me time to reach the capital that day, and now I was at Sherpur, tensely clutching my bag by the side of the road and promising Allah that I would start believing in Him if only the Dhaka bus wasn't full and I could get a seat by the window. Men hovered near me, staring intently and apparently oblivious to the evil looks I gave them. It was only ten o'clock, but the air was already as sticky as boiling syrup.

Today the jostling river town was worse than ever. It had been raining since the early morning in this, the wettest month of the monsoon, and the ugly huddle of bazaar stalls and tea-shops was virtually sinking into mud, the road which led through it churned into an unrecognisable sludge. It was a terrible time of year to be travelling. A section of the railway line to Dhaka had been immersed in flood waters for a week, and now the buses were more crowded than ever. The long line of vehicles queuing for the launch heaved and spluttered as they neared the water's edge, some getting stuck, their wheels whirring desperately as they sank deeper and deeper into the mire, and falling by the wayside as the rest of the traffic edged around them. I had already been waiting an hour for a place on one of the buses which the launch brought across from the other side of the river, and was glazed with heat and sweat. I stared despondently at the river. It was swollen and angry, carrying great tufts of vegetation and branches of trees in its fearsome current. I had never seen it so full.

'Hey, Sister! ... Oh, Katy!'

At this surprising sound of my name I looked up, and saw with pleasure that the man whom I had been studiously ignoring was a friend. It was Alim Ullah, from Talukpur. I knew his family well, and had spent many mornings sitting in their small yard, chatting to him and his brother as their one scraggy bull chewed its hay, and their mother pottered in the yard. They were cousins of the sick Abdullah, and one of the poorer households in the village; the one small patch of land they had once owned had been sold many years ago after their father's death, and now the two brothers sharecropped a few fields on the other side of the village. I often passed Alim Ullah as he worked in the fields, and he never failed to call out to me. 'Hey, Sister!' he would shout as he clicked at his bull and guided the plough behind it. 'Where are you off to today? Are you going back to London? Be sure to take me when you do!'

And now he was standing on the other side of the road, and showing off his even white teeth with his beaming grin.

'Alim Ullah! I didn't realise it was you!'

The great crowd of onlookers who had gathered around me peered at him and nudged each other at the sound of my voice. They had been speculating about me for a whole hour, talking loudly about the strange foreign woman who to all intents and purposes was travelling alone, assuming that I could not understand what they were saying. Now they saw that I could and, too, that I seemed to know the boy who had been waving at me for the past five minutes.

'What are you doing here? Are you on your way to the village?' I shouted.

'I've got business,' he declared with pride. Pulling up the ends of his trousers, he picked his way through the mud to join me on the other side of the road. Once he was standing by my side I could see that he was looking extremely smart. Rather than his usual worn lungi and vest, he was wearing trousers and a bright pink shirt. He carried an impressively full-looking bag, and his hair was oiled. His was obviously no ordinary trip across the river.

'So you're going to Sylhet?'

'No, Sister.' He continued to grin enigmatically. Why was it that I was always expected to account precisely for all my comings and goings to villagers, whilst whenever I asked where they were going they were always so vague?

'I've been in Nobiganj Town,' he said, as if this explained everything.

'And now where?'

'I'm going to Dhaka; I catch that coaster that takes you there.' He meant the manic bus that I too was waiting for, which jangled and jarred its passengers for eight hours before eventually releasing them in central Dhaka. 'And then I catch the plane that goes to the country of Allah. I'm going to Saudi.'

'What?'

'To work, Sister. I'm going to work in the land of God and grow rich.'

'You never told me about this before ... '

'I didn't have the money for my papers before, but now I've found it. It's my great chance. I'll go and work like an ox, and then we'll have the money to buy a new house, land, everything ... ' But before he had time to tell me more, the crowd began to push forward, for the launch had at last arrived. The waiting traffic shuddered towards it whilst the trucks and buses it carried edged off, honking their horns triumphantly. Alim Ullah's words were lost in a fug of petrol fumes and revving engines, and we were swept apart by the people swarming around us.

'Dhaka! Dhaka! Dhaka!'

The first bus from the launch had now jolted on to the road and was lurching towards us.

'Dhaka?' I shouted.

'Dhaka! Dhaka!' An arm swung out from the doorway and grabbed my hand, ready to pull me aboard.

'Do you have seats?'

'Seats!'

'And my friend, wait for my friend!'

But I did not need to worry, for Alim Ullah had already pushed aboard and was waving at me from the back. The bus was crammed with people so he was standing, wedged in between the narrow seats with his bag at his feet, and pressed tightly against other men who clung on to the seats and each other as the bus careered over the potholes. At this dismal sight my heart plummeted.

'No seats ... you said there were seats.'

The bus-wallah, a thin youth with a missing front tooth and a T-shirt soaked with sweat, smiled confidently at me.

'Seats, Sister!' he cried. Leaning across the row nearest to Alim Ullah, he shook a man awake and started to pull him up.

'Foreign guests!' he declared. 'Make room for our foreign visitor. She's a lady, she must sit down.'

This was exactly what I had anticipated. Other passengers were often moved for me on long journeys, so much so that I had almost begun to expect it. It would have been unthinkable to let me stand, a slur on the honour of all the other passengers, for I was not only a woman but European too, and thus of the highest status. And I never resisted my privilege. Faced with the possibility of standing for the eight-hour journey, moral scruples tended to recede.

In a somewhat pathetic gesture towards my tattered manners, I grimaced sympathetically at the uprooted man and collapsed into his seat. At last I was leaving Sylhet. I always yearned for my monthly breaks, and never was I happier in Bangladesh than when staring from bus windows at the passing scenery, watching and waiting for it to turn into the tea-gardens of Srimongol, the red soil and vegetable plots of Mymensingh, the great rivers which divided the country and took hours to cross, and eventually the hinterlands of Dhaka.

Sometimes I dozed. Then I woke with a start and peered from the window at the paddy fields and homesteads that lay beside the road. I thought of Alim Ullah, on his way to Saudi. I was not at all surprised by his news. The area had a long tradition of migration to Britain and the Gulf, and because of this it was one of the richer parts of Bangladesh, for the migrants spent their earnings on smart new houses and land, and the richest even built showy mosques and madrasas for their villages. In Talukpur, countless villagers had told me that their sons or husband were away, nodding proudly and smiling to themselves. For those who managed to get abroad and find lucrative employment, the rewards could at times be huge.

But others, in search of similar enrichment, often came home from the Middle East with virtually nothing to show for their hard work. These were the poorer men, who could not afford to pay for legal work permits and contracts, and went illegally. They entered Saudi Arabia on the pretext of doing pilgrimage at Mecca, and then hid from the authorities, dreading the deportations which would be a crushing end to their hopes. They lived in cramped rooms, in perpetual terror of the police, with hundreds of other illegal immigrants, working in all manner of jobs, which they did not talk of when they returned. They were the shoeshine boys, the cigarette sellers, the servants and manual labourers, who did the work the locals rejected and lived hard and degrading lives in their attempts to earn enough money to send to their families at home and make it all worthwhile. And now Alim Ullah was going to join them, and I would not be seeing him again. I would miss our conversations and his teasing greetings as I passed him out on the village paths. I thought of him as the bus reached another river, and wondered whether he would find the wealth he longed for.

Many of the passengers near us were talking now, shouting over the clattering of the bus and its blaring horn. I could hear Alim Ullah's voice amidst the noise. He was telling the men nearest him that he came from Talukpur, and was on his way to Saudi. Many of the others had relatives working in the Middle East. A long story was recited of someone's cousin who had a business in Kuwait, and how he had been cheated of the profits by a local. They all agreed that Saudi was very hot and dry, unlike their own country with its rivers and floods. Alim Ullah said he knew Mecca well, for had he not seen pictures of it on calendars, with the crowds of pilgrims and the tall spires of the minarets? He did not need to say that he hoped that he too would do Haj one day, and when he returned he would wear a long white robe and know Arabic. Most of all, he hoped that he would be rich.

'How are you going?' one man asked. I eyed him covertly from my seat. I did not want to attract his attention, for he looked like the type who would insist on showing off his English on me all the way to Dhaka. He carried a briefcase and had the padded, comfortable look of a townsman who had a steady wage and did not work in the fields. He was looking at Alim Ullah with distinct superiority.

'Unlegal. My friend is arranging it all.'

'And how many people are not cheated of their money by such friends who arrange their papers for them, Son? How many men fly all the way to Saudi and then are not caught by the police on their first day? Let us hope that Allah has given you a good fortune.'

But before Alim Ullah had a chance to defend the honour of his friend, the bus screeched to a halt at a roadside bazaar and the man struggled through the tightly packed bodies and climbed off. His words were indeed true. There were many stories of families who had sold all their land to send a son abroad, only to have him return within a month after being caught by the police. But Alim Ullah had to take the chance. He did not need to explain to me that he could not stay in Talukpur and do nothing but plough and harvest for the rest of his life, whilst others around him grew fat on foreign wages, for I had heard many young men like him talk of their dreams, and watched their faces when they described the riches they believed they would find abroad.

He had not told me either how it had all been arranged – I learnt of that many months later, back in Talukpur. But already I could guess, for it was the same for most would-be migrants. It had been long before the rains, when the fields were lying baked and cracked after the harvest months, that he had first discussed how he could get to Saudi. The man – for he was not really a friend – had promised to fix everything. He was a broker with much experience; he assured Alim Ullah there would be no problems. It did not matter that he had never learnt to read or write, for the broker would fill out the forms and arrange all his papers; all that was necessary was his thumbprint. He need not worry about a thing.

Alim Ullah had spent the next weeks visiting his richer relatives. He had to raise 40,000 taka (about £800) for his fares and the papers. Eventually an uncle who lived in Nobiganj agreed to give him the loan, and it was settled that Alim Ullah would pay it back from his wages. He would enter Saudi on a visitor's visa and then search for work, in hiding from the authorities. Many other men from the village would be there, and they would help him. His uncle wrote to his cousin in Mecca, and gave him his address. He had it on the bus now, tucked away in his bag with a wad of money to see him through the time he must spend in Dhaka. And that was why he had spent the last week in Nobiganj, getting the cash from his uncle and finalising arrangements with the broker, who had given him an address in Dhaka, a boarding-house where he could be found and where Alim Ullah could stay.

'It's my cousin's hotel,' the broker had told him. 'You only have to ask for me. Everyone there knows who I am.'

He promised that they would meet there and take the same flight to Saudi. He would show him where to go when they arrived, and make sure he found a place to stay. He had left for Dhaka a few days earlier, and promised Alim Ullah that he would be waiting there for him.

As the day wore on and I grew sticky with heat and blurred with fatigue, the bus began to leave the Sylheti countryside behind. Here there was less water, and further on the soil was a different shade. I peered for a full hour at the tea-gardens we crossed, watching the groups of plantation workers swarm over the bush-covered hills. They were foreign women from Orissa and Bihar, far darker than the Sylheti locals, with rings in their noses and baskets on their backs. Some of them had been born on their plantations, and would never leave. By mid afternoon we were far from Talukpur, and everything which was familiar.

After the tea-gardens the day grew dark again and rain began to splatter against the windows, smearing the view and seeping in to form a dirty pool of water on the floor. The road ahead grew hazy in the downpour, but instead of slowing the bus increased in speed, careering through the puddles as if to escape the wet. For miles now there had been nothing but water, the road a dry spine raised up through the endless flood lands. In the distance, great fishing nets were spread across the water. Sometime, we passed small boats crowded with people moving slowly out towards the horizon. If there had ever been villages there, they had disappeared.

'Ya Allah, such rains we're having!' my neighbours were saying. 'The whole of this area is underwater, they were talking of it on the radio.'

'There's a great flood?'

'Brother! I've never seen the waters like this before. They say thousands of people have lost their homes in the South.'

'And the railway line's broken too,' said another man. 'We were going to take the train this morning, but no, there's been no trains since last night. The whole line was swept away by the river, for about two miles.'

'But the road's good?'

'Allah willing. But who knows? In this rain, it can't stay like that for long. It was closed a month ago for a whole week.'

I said nothing, but began to pray again. The last time I had gone to Dhaka the road had been broken, and there had been no alternative but to take our luggage from the bus and wade through the torrent until we reached dry land and another bus. Not only had this been scary but it had taken hours, and I was anxious to get to Dhaka before it grew too late. I could not wait to reach my expatriate friends' huge and beautiful house, open a bottle of beer and read the mail which I hoped more than anything had been accumulating for me since I had last left for Talukpur.

My prayers were answered, for soon we reached the great Megna River, and although it was filled with the brown water of floods and rushed ferociously beneath the launch, on the other side the landscape grew progressively drier. We were growing close to Dhaka now, and the bus slowly began to empty. Alim Ullah at last found himself a seat opposite mine, wedged between an elderly man who snored loudly and eventually dropped his head on to his neighbour's shoulder, and a basket of ducks. After a while I noticed that he too had fallen asleep.

The bus clattered into Dhaka just as the city's mosques began the sunset call to prayer. There were no floods here yet; merely giant puddles through which the traffic splashed easily. It did not even seem to have been raining. Instead, a few lingering rays of golden light fell across the cluttered skyline of breeze-block buildings, decorated minarets and factory chimneys. Already lights were showing in windows and the tea-stalls shone with lamps.

The road leading to the bus station was choked with crazed traffic going in all directions, and the trucks and taxis, baby-taxis and rickshaws appeared irredeemably tangled together in a hopeless knot. The blasé trucks, with might on their side, merely blared their horns and forged ahead, unchallengeable giants with 'Allah is Great' and pictures of rustic scenes painted on their flanks. The baby-taxis squealed their hooters and attempted to squeeze their way through the mêlée, whilst from time to time irritated drivers lost their cool completely and, slamming their car doors behind them, set about slapping a rickshaw driver who was in their way.

As always after a stint in the village, Dhaka seemed vast and slightly threatening. Ludicrously, since I had spent almost all my life in London, the city vaguely shocked me. I noticed two girls in a rickshaw laughing. They were wearing shalwar kameez, and their heads were uncovered. Their hair was bobbed; bright dangly ornaments hung from their ears. Other women walked alone, without burquas or umbrellas, yet they were surely not poor, for their saris were made of silk. There were beggars too, lying stretched out on the pavements and squatting by the drains while the crowds brushed past them. On the other side of the road were shops with great pyramids of sweetmeats stacked in the windows, or fancy saris and shalwars displayed on plastic mannequins. Others blared Hindi film music, which blended into the roar of horns and engines and people shouting. A couple of cows wandered indolently by the side of the road, munching garbage and occasionally stealing fruit from the stalls as they passed. My insides churned in excitement. Dhaka! Freedom! The joys of expatriate life!

When at last the bus stopped, I fought my way off and found Alim Ullah standing in the middle of the bus station, a small figure in the centre of the chaos. My legs were shaking from the cramped journey, and my head beat in a steady pulse of pain. I smiled weakly at him.

'So, we're here.'

He looked smaller and more insignificant than I could ever have imagined in Talukpur. People jostled him and shouted angrily if he blocked their way. His new shirt and trousers were crumpled and dirty from the day – splattered with mud, and soggy with sweat.

'Acha. I'm going now.'

We stood facing each other as the other passengers shoved past us. Like them, I was eager to be on my way. My back and legs ached from the uncomfortable bus seats, and my shalwar kameez was sticking unpleasantly to my skin. I wanted to have a shower, speak English, switch off for a while. I longed to be off to the oasis of mansions on the other side of the city where many of the aid workers lived. In the roar of the bus station, with cement rather than Talukpur soil beneath my feet, I was a different person, no longer the village *beti* of twelve hours earlier. Outside the boundaries of the village I had shifted my identity. Here in Dhaka I was Western again.

'You'll come with me, Sister, to my hotel to eat rice with me?'

'It's getting so late, I really have to go.'

'Sister, how can we travel all the way to Dhaka and you not even come and drink tea with me?' He was smiling winningly.

I sighed, sensing that however much I wanted to complete my transformation and get to my beer and letters, he would probably succeed in persuading me.

'Where is your hotel, then?'

He continued to grin. 'I have the address, here, written down.'

He rummaged in his shirt pocket and eventually produced a sweaty piece of paper with Bengali writing on it.

'I can't read this, I'm illiterate.'

It was quite true, I had never mastered written Bengali. None the less, whenever I spoke of myself in this way it always raised a laugh.

'What does it say, then?'

He stared fixedly at it and then shrugged. 'I don't understand it.'

'You can't read either?'

'I thought you'd be able to tell me the way, Sister.'

'Well look, you can ask someone here.'

He shuffled his feet and stared gloomily at the ground.

'Ya Allah, what's the matter?'

'Sister, I'm ashamed.'

Alim Ullah stood before me, completely changed. Only a few days earlier I had sat and listened while he patiently answered my questions on village agriculture, the soil, the plants that grew around his homestead, the different fish that swam in the river. Afterwards he had let me record the songs which he and the other poorer men sang as they worked in the fields. They were of the saints, of love and the glory of Allah, of the golden land of Bengal. He was only about twenty-three, but in his lungi, his feet bare, he was more mature and wise than any of my university-educated men friends back in Britain. Now all this had gone. He stood in the middle of the bus station in his badly fitting trousers which ended at his ankles, plastic shoes, and the bright pink shirt which his family had stored for special occasions since the 1970s. He did not know where he was going because he could not read. Here, to the people who pushed around him, he was an illiterate village oaf.

'Look, I'll get a baby-taxi.'

I strode purposefully towards a gaggle of parked scooters. The drivers gathered around me as I approached, nudging each other and laughing at the sight of the foreign woman who no doubt could be charged double the price.

'Madam! Yes Madam!' They cried out in English.

'Where's this? We can't read.' I handed them the paper, trying to look as Bengali as possible. Once I could demonstrate that I was not a total innocent, the inevitable battle over prices would be partially won.

'Yysh! Listen to her! She speaks our words!'

A large man with a great belly and long white beard wiped his hands on his lungi and grabbed my arm. 'You've learnt our Bengali words!'

The others were all nodding and grinning now. It was a scene I went through each time I hired a baby-taxi.

'And you thought I was foreign and stupid. So now you know I'm not, you can't cheat me.'

The drivers paused doubtfully. Then they worked out the meaning of my garbled Sylheti and laughed, repeating it for each other. It never failed. I always made the same joke, and the response never differed.

'Did you hear her? She said we thought she was stupid!'

They were laughing, of course, because it was true. The driver with the white beard handed back the paper.

'Farmgate,' he said. It was a large, busy area on the way to the airport.

'How much?'

'Thirty taka.'

'Twenty.'

He paused and then, in the ritual conclusion of a haggle, inclined his head slightly to the back seat of the scooter.

'Great!' I grabbed my bag and, quite inappropriately, Alim Ullah's arm, and pulled him into the baby-taxi.

With a splutter the scooter came alive and began to push its way into the busy road, in the direction where the confusion seemed to increase in intensity. The sun had set now, and the sky had turned violet. A smear of smoke and fumes lay furled on the horizon. Although the day had been clear, there were no stars. Clutching our seats as the baby-taxi bumped and swerved, we passed over a railway track and turned off the road into a labyrinth of alleys lined with traders selling huge piles of fruit and vegetables, or sitting among great baskets filled with rice or lentils. Sometimes the line of stalls ended and the road veered close to the railway line, cutting through huddles of huts built from plastic sheets and sacking. Then it pulled away, back towards the main road, before we could fully register the stench of poverty. At last we turned a corner in the small backstreet, and came to a huge road roaring with traffic. Far ahead was a footbridge which, like the pavements below, was teeming with people and beggars.

'Farmgate,' declared our driver, turning round and smiling radiantly at us.

'Mother! Watch the road!' I screamed in his ear.

He laughed and abruptly turned off the main street into another side road, slowing the baby-taxi until it stopped as it had started – with a sad splutter. Facing us was a decrepit shop front with a sign declaring

'Dentist's Surgery'. That this was indeed so was proved by a large painting of the insides of a mouth, complete with teeth, gums, jawbones and a protruding tongue. The driver pointed to the storey above the surgery. Here, another sign proclaimed: 'Majestic Hotel'.

'That's your hotel.'

'Acha. Now I'm going somewhere else ... How much to Gulshan?' But Alim Ullah did not move.

'Sister, you must still drink tea with me. I shall introduce you to my friend. He will be so happy to meet you.'

'Yes, I'd really like it,' I lied, 'but I have to go. The azan's sounded and it'll be dark soon.'

I wanted desperately to be inside the air-conditioned walls of the house on the other side of town, to step out of my sticky clothes and into a shower.

'Sister, if you don't come in I'll know you don't care about me. I'll be in Saudi soon, and when I come back you'll be in London. We shan't ever be able to talk again.'

It was pure village blackmail. It had been used on me many times before, and would be used many times again. It always worked.

'Acha. OK. Come on then.'

I gave our driver his twenty taka and we pushed the door, which opened on to stairs up to the hotel. At the top we came to a dingy hallway, dominated by an imposing-looking reception desk. A man was sitting at it, smoking and listening to the news on a crackling radio. He did not look up as we appeared, but muttered, 'We're full'.

'Is this the Majestic Hotel?'

'Full,' the man repeated, and spat on the floor. He was wearing a crumpled suit and a pair of dark glasses – for reasons of fashion, it would seem, rather than comfort, for the bulb over the desk threw out a sickly yellow light which did not reach the corridor leading away from the hall. There was a smear of black on his forehead; in the heat his hair dye had started to run.

'But I'm looking for my friend.'

He ignored Alim Ullah, and glanced at me.

'No rooms,' he said in English.

'I don't want a room,' I replied, in the most upper-class Bengali accent I could muster.

'No rooms! No women allowed! This hotel for businessmen!'

The more patronising and authoritarian a man was, it so often seemed, the more likely he was to insist on English.

'Yes, I know, but I don't want to stay here.'

The man spat again and looked away, dismissing us.

'Patronising git.' If he wanted English, he would get it. I smiled sweetly at him. He ignored me.

'Eh, Abdul! Bring me more cigarettes!' He tossed a note across the desk and a young boy appeared from the shadows, slipping the money into his vest as he scuttled off down the stairs.

'So where's your friend, then?' I said, turning to Alim Ullah.

'Here, here. He will most certainly be coming, any minute.'

He took a step forward, coughing to attract the hotelier's attention.

'Sir, I am searching for my friend who is staying here. He said everyone here would know him. I have to meet him.'

'So what's his name?'

'Saiyed Mohammed Ahmed. He's from the village of Kandiganj in Nobiganj. My name is Alim Ullah from Talukpur. Do you know him?'

There was a pause. The man began to prepare a large wad of pan, filling it with betel and spices as he studiously avoided Alim Ullah's eye.

'Yes, I know him.'

'And where is he?'

'I don't know where he is. He's not here. Now go away!'

He was using the informal '*tumi*', addressing Alim Ullah as he might a servant or rickshaw driver. It was terribly insulting.

'But he has all my papers. We arranged it. I'm going to Saudi ... he's been helping me.'

'I don't know where he is. Ysssh, this heat! Can't that fan go any faster? ... So why are you still here? Didn't you hear? I don't know where Mohammed Ahmed is.'

'But he has my money!'

'Yes, yes, he has everyone's money. I can't do anything, so you might as well go away.'

'But I have to find him. That's 40,000 taka! He must be here!' Alim Ullah had begun to shout, and his hands were shaking. I did not understand most of what he said now, but could hear the words 'money' and 'Saudi', and the despair in his voice. The hotelier stared back at him impassively, belching occasionally in small, noisy eruptions. The betel nut seemed to have disagreed with his digestion. Eventually

Alim Ullah's outburst began to falter and he grew silent. The man sighed wearily.

'Acha,' he said. He was obviously accustomed to such scenes. 'If you must know, your business partner's gone. He was here last week, but now he's left. He flew to Kuwait last week.'

He gave one last, resplendent belch, and once more picked up his newspaper. There was nothing more to be said.

I stood, horrified, behind Alim Ullah. He had obviously been cheated. I did not know what to do. I could hardly leave him, yet I could hardly help him either. He could not come back to my friends' house with me. That would have been quite inappropriate, especially since he did not even come from my village household. In this new context of the city, it hardly seemed right for us to be calling each other 'Brother' and 'Sister'.

'What will you do?' I asked him. 'Can I help you? Would you like my telephone number in Dhaka?'

He smiled. 'What good will that be? It's not a problem. This is a very bad man, with a lying tongue. I know my friend hasn't gone to Kuwait. I'll find him. You should go now.'

'Acha.'

We stood awkwardly facing each other. I did not know how to say goodbye, either. Village people never shook hands, and they never kissed. I lunged forward, and pressed my nose against his. It was terribly brazen, but I knew he would understand. After all, my naive breaches of propriety were a common joke in the village. We exchanged the Arabic leavetaking.

'*Kuddha Hafis.*'

'*Kuddha Hafis.*'

I picked up my things and quickly walked back down the stairs, leaving Alim Ullah standing alone in the dim reception area, with his muddy trousers and his bag at his feet.

A whole week later, I was on my way back to Talukpur. The day had already begun to fade as my boat approached the village, and dusk was falling as swiftly as the rain. Although it was only about five miles from the road, the journey had taken hours. In some places the river had overflowed its banks completely, taking over the fields and villages which usually lay beyond it. The rain kept up for the whole journey, drumming down on my umbrella and the plastic bag which the boatman had pulled over his head, and splashing into the water. As we got closer to Talukpur, I began to recognise familiar landmarks. The river-bank was still intact, but beyond it the fields, which a week earlier had been merely swampy, were now totally submerged, and the paths which led across them disintegrated into ragged patches of grass, showing only occasionally through the water. The world had turned to sea and the baris rising from it were islands, marooned in the grey.

At last we rounded the corner in the river which led into the village. Far over on one side I could see my own bari, surrounded by its tall mango trees and the patch of jute which grew at the front, by the river's edge. On the other side, we had begun to pass the first huts spread along the banks. These were the poorest, for here the land was lower and they were on the margins of the village. First were the ramshackle huts of Wahed Ullah, and then the small, battered homestead of Abdullah. The boatman sat back on his heels and lit a bedi as the current took us past them.

The village seemed eerily deserted, even though it was still light. An hour later, in the uneasy interval between sunset and night, when the sky turned purple and then deep blue and the birds were screeching in the rain, the villagers would light their lamps and bolt their doors against the dark. These were the dangerous hours, Amma and Sufia had told me many times, just after the sun had disappeared, when evil spirits roamed free. I was lucky that I had made it back in time, for no boatman would take me down the river in the dark.

'Katy!'

I took my umbrella away from my face, and saw that we had reached the bari of Alim Ullah. In the week I had been in Dhaka, he had receded from my thoughts. As always, everything to do with the village seemed very distant when I was away from it, just as did everything outside it when I was there. Now, I was reminded painfully of when I had last seen him.

'Oh, Beti! Come here!'

Standing in front of the soggy fence of banana leaves which surrounded the cluster of huts was Alim Ullah's mother, Santi Bibi. She was beckoning at me furiously, waving her thin arms in the air and calling out my name.

'Stop for a minute, Beti, just to show us that you care. Our roof is broken; don't you want to see that? If you loved us you would.'

Emotional blackmail was obviously a family speciality. I also wanted to find out what had happened to Alim Ullah. I told the boatman to pull over to the bank whilst I paid my call, and clambered up the slippery slope towards Santi Bibi. She took my arm, and pulled me up.

'Haven't you heard?' she was saying. 'We've had terrible rains, and our bari's been broken. My brother Abdullah's home is flooded as well, the water's come right inside.'

'Inside? So what are they doing?'

'They've gone. They went to Kakura this morning to stay with that cousin of theirs. My niece is at your aunt's place, sleeping with Sufia.'

'So my bari isn't flooded?'

'No, girl.' The old woman jerked her head over to the other side of the river. 'They're the lucky ones.'

As we entered the enclosure of Alim Ullah's bari, I saw what had happened. The yard was full of water, not from the river but from the fields which lay behind. Bits of debris floated desolately in front of us – a plastic shoe, a plank, pieces from a broken pot.

'Look,' said Santi Bibi, her voice shaky with emotion, 'the kitchen's broken'.

Although the front rooms of the homestead were still intact, at the back the flimsy building was broken into a derelict pile. The walls of the kitchen area had fallen into the water and the makeshift thatch roof was leaning beside them. The back of the bari had simply crumpled in, like a card house in a breeze.

'Ya Allah!' I said, as the water lapped around my ankles. 'Your son isn't here?'

'Here? Oh no, he's in Saudi.'

'Saudi ... ' I muttered vaguely. He had obviously not yet returned from Dhaka. I would have to tell her what had happened. I knew I could not do it then. It would have to be the next day, when I was feeling braver.

'Yes, Beti, that's right. My son is going to be there for many years. God has taken him so that he can work and send us money. It's His will. You must pray for him.' She was smiling now. 'It's a great thing for us. Isn't that the only way we will ever get any wealth? How can we survive if we just sharecrop the land like paupers? And now the bari's broken with this angry water, we have to build another one. We couldn't do that without his earnings.'

She pulled her sari over her head and glanced towards the river, and the mosque. 'Allah has been merciful to us. Even though I cry for my boy, it's our good fortune that the Lord has taken him away. By the will of God, our lives will get better.'

And with this thought the old woman squeezed my hand and smiled at me, for despite all the stories of cheats, deportation and broken dreams, she was sure that their fortunes must soon change. Tomorrow, Alim Ullah would be flying to the land of Allah, to make them money and change their lives. It was the only way they would edge from poverty, and with all her heart, with every inch of her being, she really believed that it was so.

It was not until a month later that Alim Ullah finally returned. He came back by boat, the way he had gone, in the same bright pink shirt and the same badly fitting trousers. I was sitting by the river with Mobed and the other little boys when I saw him.

'Look! It's Alim Ullah!' I jumped up and waved.

'Hey, Alim Ullah!' Mobed cried out at him. 'Why have you come back? We thought you were in Saudi!'

He giggled and nudged me. I had told the family what had happened, but rather than share my horror, or express sympathy, they had laughed at their poorer cousin's stupidity.

Now Alim Ullah had seen us too. He turned and shouted at us across the water.

'I had some problems! But I've seen all the sights of Dhaka, and I'll be going to Saudi next year. Just wait and see, I have many plans!'

But at this Mobed laughed even louder, and blew a raspberry. Like everyone in the village, he had heard such stories many times before.

11 AMBIA'S STORY

My belly full of rice and fish and my back dripping with sweat, I was lying under my mosquito net writing yet another letter. The evening call to prayer had long been over now, and at last the soggy air was cooling. More rain was promised, too, by the distant roars of thunder and flashes of blue light across the dark sky. Outside, the monotonous chirp of crickets was punctuated only by the croak of toads, those great heavy beasts which leapt around my room and into my path as I stumbled to the latrine in the night. In the next room I could hear the gurgle of Abba's hookah, and clatters from the kitchen as his rice was prepared for him. It was a typical village night in the rainy season.

'Are you sleeping, Elder Sister?'

A face suddenly appeared from the damp gloom of the room, and was peering into my net. As quietly as the evening rain, now beginning at last, a guest had joined me.

'I've come to look at you. How you write! You must be so clever!' My visitor stood uncertainly by the bed, watching the door nervously.

'No, I'm stupid. I can't do anything useful. I can't even cook rice properly. Anyway, you could easily write if you'd been taught.'

I pulled up my net and gave the young woman standing in front of me my hand. 'Don't you want to sit down?'

She looked at the door again, fearful of being caught by anyone in the family, and then sat down on the wooden slats.

'Where's your daughter?'

'Sleeping. She's been crying all day from bellyache, but now she's quiet. Yah Allah, I'm so tired, every bit of me hurts!'

My visitor was called Ambia; she worked in our household as a servant.

Ambia and her little girl first came to the bari whilst I was away in Sylhet. When I eventually got back, there they were, hanging in the

126

background as the rest of the family clustered round to hear my news and see the things I had brought them from the town. She was one of many servant women who drifted in and out of the richer village households. Some stayed only for the day, hurrying off at dusk with a small bundle of rice wrapped in their saris as their wages. Others stayed for months, sometimes even years if a household had enough work, and could afford to hire them.

Many of the women who worked in Talukpur came from outside the district, travelling for days on launches and buses from their own villages to this richer part of the country. 'Our land has gone now,' they would tell me. 'It was taken by the river waters.' Others said they had always worked as servants, had never known a time when their families had their own fields and their mothers and aunts did not have to go from village to village in search of employment. But many of the servant women were local too, often walking to villages only a few miles over the fields in the dry season so that they would not be shamed by people in their own village seeing them, and knowing that they had to face the humiliation of working in another family's bari. Ambia was one of these.

'What's the name of your new beti?' I asked Amma as she inspected a length of cloth I had brought her from Sylhet.

'Ambia. Katy, you're a fool to have paid fifty taka for this.'

'How long has she been here?'

'She came last Friday, Daughter. Yysh! And how much did you pay for this blouse? That colour will run ... '

At first Ambia was too shy to speak to me. She would stand and watch as I wrote my diary on the verandah, or washed my clothes at the ghat, but only shook her head if I said anything to her. Her little girl, who continually hovered near me staring with great curious eyes, ran giggling to her mother if I spoke. But it did not take long to make them into friends.

'Do you have rice in your country, Elder Sister?' Ambia asked a few evenings after I'd arrived, as I ate my meal in the kitchen and she stirred the rice pot. They were the first words she had dared to address to me.

'It doesn't grow there, but we buy it from other countries. And Ambia, if you call me "Elder Sister" I'll feel sad, because we're equal, and actually you're older than me.'

'You don't eat much of it ... Elder Sister, are you married?'

'No ... Ambia, I'm going to give your daughter my food, they've given me far too much again.'

Her little girl usually ate at the same time as me, far earlier than the household women, whom I never had the patience to join, for they sat down to their meal only after all the men and visitors had been served, sometimes as late as ten or eleven o'clock. The child's dish was always pitifully empty, and she never got the fish or vegetables from the family pot which were piled on to my plate. Away from Amma's watchful eyes, the skinny child was rapidly becoming an invaluable way of avoiding daily overstuffing.

'You should make Shiria eat more of the vegetables,' I told Ambia. 'They'll help her to grow.'

It was not a particularly helpful remark, for Ambia had little choice in what she and Shiria ate. The local custom of eating huge mounds of rice with only a spoonful of chutney, or a little gravy from the curry, was not one born of preference; the fish and vegetables that I enthu-siastically tucked into were by far the most expensive foods, and few village households could afford to eat them in large quantities. Servants in the village were given as much rice as they wanted, but the pots of curry sitting by the fire were another matter. Ambia said nothing, but watched approvingly as her child ate. I sensed that she wanted to ask me something, but did not have the courage.

'Elder Sister, do you have any of your powder for heat?' she said at last. 'My little Shiria's been crying from her heat rash all day.'

And so I gave Ambia my tin of anti-heat-rash powder, and from that moment on we were firm friends.

Ambia was probably in her late twenties. She had a sweet round face, warm brown eyes, and hands as rough as old leather. Her features had been inherited from her mother, and her hands were the result of all the hours she had spent grinding spices, collecting dung for fuel, pounding rice to powder, sweeping, cleaning, washing, and all the thousand other tasks that filled her days and made her bones ache for sleep. She had worked for many years in the villages around her home as a servant and was used to spending her life in other women's kitchens, cleaning up after families which were not her own. When asked, she said that she could not remember how long her life had been like that, for the months and years had merged, and she had never counted them.

She was always the first to get up in the mornings, woken by the sounds of the cocks crowing, or the azan. Then she would shake Shiria awake, and the two quietly creep into the kitchen where she would light the fire, soak the previous evening's rice and then take the dirty pots down to the dawn-lit pond to wash them. Shiria always followed her like a shadow, shivering in the cold morning fog.

From then until late into the night, Ambia worked ceaselessly. She cleaned the cowsheds of manure, and patted it out to dry in the sun; she remade the mud floors and walls of the house; she spent long hours grinding and pounding, or bent over a da, shredding and cutting vegetables and fish. She washed and swept, and cooked and brought in firewood, and when she had finished that she cared for little Shiria, carefully combing out her matted hair and bathing her in the pond with a sliver of soap used by the rest of us for washing clothes. She ate after everybody else, squatting with Shiria over the tin plate they were given, sharing the remnants of the family pot. At night, when the last dish of rice had been served and the kitchen fire burnt down, she sometimes laid the little girl on the mat and then quietly joined the bari women to hear their talk and tell them of her own family, if they would listen.

Her village was about two miles away from Talukpur, an hour's walk into the green landscape. Through the paddy, past a straggling village, over a creaky bamboo bridge, and then, in the distance, a long line of mud and thatch baris appeared. Amongst them was Ambia's home. The only stone building there was the mosque, for unlike many of the villages around it, all its inhabitants were poor; even the richest family owned only a few fields. They had always been poor, although memories were not long enough to stretch back to explanations. The oldest man in the village, who no longer left his hut but sat outside it muttering in the sun, said the British made it like that, many years before his birth, and how could they ever hope to buy land now, when it was in such demand and so expensive?

Ambia and her mother had once owned a separate hut with a room for cooking, a wooden bed, and a stand for their clothes. But a year earlier their lamp had been knocked over, setting the room on fire and burning it to a charred stub, along with most of their possessions. So now they stayed in a small thatch room at the edge of a cousin's bari. They had two mats, a worn pillow, a row of pots and a clay fire

in one corner. The women each had two saris, and Shiria had a pair
of knickers and a torn dress. But everything was clean – scrupulously
so – and far tidier than the large and chaotic household in which I lived.

Ambia told me her story that evening, as the rain pattered down on
the tin roof and Abba snored. The family did not like her to talk with
me, and accused her of skiving if she slipped into my room and sat
down on my bed, so she came only if she thought they wouldn't see.
But still, we were able to spend many hours together, talking in
whispers in the lamplight or sitting out at the back of the bari as I bathed
and she washed the family's clothes. Anyway, tonight Amma and Najma
had gone to stay at the bari of Amma's father, so there were fewer
watchful eyes to note Ambia's absence from the kitchen.

'So do you want to hear of my sadnesses, then?' she began. 'Elder
Sister, it's not a beautiful story. What can I tell you?'

'Explain everything to me, so that one day I'll be able to tell people
in my country about women like you, and they'll be able to understand
a bit more.'

'And then will they send money for my daughter and mother?'

'No, they won't do that, but perhaps some people will be able to
help in other ways … '

It was a hollow promise, and my vague statements about 'world
understanding' always sounded ridiculous and irrelevant when I tried
them out on village people, who knew far better than I did that such
cosy Western ideas were not going to do them much good. Ambia
looked suitably unconvinced, but was too polite to voice her disap-
pointment.

'I was born in that village over there,' she started, jerking her head
as if this would explain everything. 'I don't know when it was – before
the Independence war. My father was poor; he was a labourer. He
died when I was still drinking at my *ammazie's* breasts. I don't remember
him at all. I had four brothers, all older than me, but since they've
taken their own wives they have to look after them, they can't help
me. They work, too, on fields owned by other families. That's always
been the way for our family. Our Allah didn't mean for us to be wealthy,
that wasn't the way He made for us, so what can we do? We say that
wealth is nothing but a test for the rich. If they give it away, then good,
they'll please Our Lord on the Day of Judgement, but if they take the
other path, then they'll go to hell. We don't have such temptations

as them. Do you understand what I'm saying? For us poor, what can we do but pray for things to get better? Elder Sister, will you give me some of your pan?' I gave her a big wad of betel nut wrapped with *jorda* (sweetened tobacco) into the spicy leaf, and she pushed it luxuriously into her mouth.

'I can't talk for long, they'll be calling me back to work soon ... Yah Allah, you gave me so much jorda!' Ambia spat the pan out in a great red blob and, wiping her mouth on her sari, carried on with her story.

'My family gave me away in marriage when I was very small. I was not much bigger than my Shiria then. No, I forget – maybe thirteen? Only educated people remember things like that. They took me away from my ammazie to another village in the east. You can't know how much I cried! You're not married yet, but when you are, you'll know what it is to cry for your parents.'

'It's different in my country.'

'Have your parents already arranged a husband for you? Will he be rich? I'll pray for you that he'll be such a rich man, and learned too, like you!'

'Actually, we don't have arranged marriages like you. Ambia, will you tell me about your husband?'

'What can I say to you? After I'd cried for a few weeks, I began to love him. I did everything for him. I gave him all his food, until he wouldn't take it from anyone but me, not even his mother. I lit his bedis for him, and only then would he smoke them. Not seeing him was like death for me, and then when he was there, I was alive. What else is there to tell you? Isn't marriage the same in your country? Then my little Shiria made my belly big, and she was born. Those days, I had much happiness in my life. Shiria's father gave her more love than I can tell you of ... He carried her around the bari, singing such beautiful songs to her, and brought bananas from the bazaar to feed her with. If she dirtied herself then he'd take her right down to the river-side to wash her, as if it was his stomach that had carried her. Yah Allah, how times go and change!'

'Did he die, Ambia?'

'No, he didn't die, he went away.' She looked down to her hands again. The rain was beating hard on the roof, and had already begun to drip steadily on to the mud floor.

'My Shiria came and the years went by, but there were no more babies, no sons for his family. After Shiria, you see, there had been nothing – a baby had started inside me, but it died, and then I'd been ill, and my body was ruined. Do you understand what I'm saying? Then one day he took another woman. He came to me and told me I was black and ugly, and there was another woman he wanted who could give him a son. He said, would I agree to go back to my village? He didn't have the money to support two wives. I cried, saying I wouldn't go, that he was Shiria's abazie, and what could we do without him? So he beat me hard, until I could hardly walk. Everybody saw it, but they didn't do anything. Shiria's father is very strong, and he gets very angry.'

'So what did you do?'

'After he had beaten me he went off, saying that if I refused to get out he'd go himself. He would go to his new wife's village. That was how I understood it. All that night I stayed awake, crying and praying. I thought maybe he had gone to the bazaar, but he didn't return with food for our meal, so there was nothing to eat. My Shiria just slept, she was only a baby then. I didn't dare go to my husband's relatives, I was too ashamed, but they all knew that he had gone. So when the first azan began, I got up and we crept out of the village, before anyone was awake and could see us. It was the cold season, and my heart was freezing over, Elder Sister. We walked all morning. His village was many miles from mine. I walked until every part of me was hot with pain, and my head was throbbing, *boom, boom, boom.* Then I could see the huts of my father's village, and its mosque, the country of my birth.

'When I got there everyone in our bari came out. "Have you come on a visit?" they all asked. "Why hasn't Shiria's abba come with you?" I was too shy to say anything, but they all knew what had happened. If my husband had cared for me he wouldn't have let me walk alone like that, would he? At first my amma didn't speak, she just gave me rice and didn't ask me any questions. We didn't talk about anything until late in the night, when everyone else was sleeping.

'"Your fate's turned out bad, Daughter," she said. "He's a bad one, I felt it from the start. I've heard lots of talk about those in-laws of yours."

'We sat outside – it was winter then, so there was no mud – and talked like you and I are talking now.

'"We'll manage, Daughter," she said to me. "Allah has returned you to me, and given me back my little granddaughter, and if that's the way He wills it, then so be it. I'm poor, but I'll give you what I can. Even if that son-in-law comes back for you, I won't let him take you now."

'And so I stayed there, where I live now. Elder Sister, if you come and visit me there, I'll be able to cook for you, and you can see my family and my bari! When will you come?'

'Oh, Ambia, after the worst of the rains. It's not a good time for walking now.'

'Acha. Shall I tell more of my story?'

I passed her some more pan, this time without the offending jorda, and Ambia picked up my fan, creaking it slowly around above us so that it gently stirred the heavy air.

'Years passed. How can I say how many? My Shiria grew taller, but her abba never came to see her. Still today he hasn't come; he's forgotten us. So, years passed, and we had no money. How can you eat without that? Can you fill your belly on air? So now I work like a slave for other people. You've seen it all.'

'How much do they pay you?'

Ambia's voice dropped to a whisper. 'I work all the month, every day, and after that I get fifty taka [about £1], and they give me my rice. Sometimes my baby comes with me, sometimes they say, "No, we can't feed her too, she must stay at home." So my mother cares for her. And then how can I survive? Without her, I might as well be dead ... If I wake in the night, and she's not beside me, I can't sleep again. But what can I do? Everything has been ordered by Allah, so how can I change it? Perhaps next year I'll get sick, and then we'll just be beggars ... My life is so full of sadness, but I must keep on, isn't that true? And Sister, have you heard the way they shout at me here? That other sister, that Najma, she's always telling me: do this, do that, and shouting that they'll send me away because my work doesn't please them. All day long, nothing but fighting. Have you seen?'

She was certainly right. The family women were harsh judges of the work of servants, and drove them hard. I suppose women like Ambia often become the scapegoats for their employers' own frustrations and weariness.

'I wish I could do something about it; it makes me very sad when I hear them shouting at you.'

'You could tell them not to.'

'That would only make them more angry.'

I had tried this tactic of defending servant women before, and the result had been disastrous. 'You don't understand, Katy!' I had been told. 'How can you tell when you don't know what it's like to work with these women? Are you saying our family isn't good? Is that it?'

And so I had decided that it was better to say nothing, for not only was my understanding of the situation incomplete, but it inevitably seemed to make it worse for the woman concerned.

'Yah Allah,' Ambia suddenly said, 'now they're calling me, and I'm really going to get scolded for talking so long'.

And pulling her tattered sari over her head, she got up and hurried back into the kitchen.

The rain continued all night, and I lay awake for hours thinking about what Ambia had told me. She was by no means the only woman who had such a story. Many poor women came to see me in the hope of a free sari or some taka, having heard that there was a rich foreign girl in Talukpur. During the day, bari rooms are open for anyone to wander in, and I would often open my eyes to an unknown and usually tightly pinched face peering down curiously at me, and the words, 'Have you woken, Auntie?' Sometimes when I told them I wasn't a walking charity and anyway, had only three saris myself, they disappeared. But others would sit down and talk, and I learnt much from them.

Ambia's position was by no means the worst, although she was closer than many to the dread of total impoverishment, and having to rely on alms to fill her small family pot with rice.

Every day the bari was visited by destitute women asking for alms. They were instantly recognisable with their ragged saris and bare feet, and rough sacks to carry the rice they were given. I was soon to become accustomed to their cry of 'Yah Allah, give me charity!' which was always uttered with their calling card of a long, mournful sigh. Almsgiving is an integral part of the Muslim faith, and unless the family stocks were seriously low, the women would always eventually be rewarded by a small basket of rice placed on the verandah steps for them to pick up at a respectful distance.

The men who came never entered the inner yard, but stood by the outer buildings sighing and crying until eventually they caught somebody's attention. They were usually old and looked pathetically broken, with their slow jagged steps and linecarved faces. Some of them sang religious songs and sported frayed prayer caps, and if they were lucky the whole bari would come out to listen to their pious verses. Others, more pedlars than beggars, toured the baris with chained monkeys, or performed dances with sticks, which they whirred over their heads as they writhed their bodies around, much to everyone's amusement.

Like the beggars outside the village, who lived at the railway stations and river crossings, some of the people who wandered around the neighbourhood collecting alms were dreadfully deformed, their illnesses or disabilities having become their livelihoods. One woman appeared with a strange, jerky walk and a manic twitch, her face distorted with spasms so that everyone ran inside screeching in horror when they saw her. Another young girl had a huge growth on her nose which had taken over most of her face, submerging her features in what seemed like the trunk of an elephant. The bari women gave her several taka in stunned silence for her misfortune.

But the majority of beggars were simply people who had reached the bottom rung in life: old men with no land, and without kin to care for them; the sick, or women who had been widowed or abandoned by their menfolk and now had no alternative but to hold out their dishes and cry 'Allah!', often carrying their babies and toddlers with them as they walked from bari to bari. Sometimes I would meet them outside the bari, or down at the family ghat, as they rested or washed themselves. 'What is your country?' they would ask after a surprised pause. 'Are your parents of this bari?' These exchanges often did not get far, for I usually had great difficulty understanding their non-Talukpur accents, and they stared in blankness at my garbled rendition of their language.

Sometimes there were vast congregations of local destitute people in the village. At a funeral, or if word had got around that a sacrifice was going to be made and the meat of the bull distributed to the poor, they would arrive in their hundreds, walking over the fields to the bari in which it was going to take place and then sitting patiently and quietly, sometimes all day, until they were rewarded with a small lump of gristle or a handful of rice.

No one paid them any attention as they passed on the village paths. These were the '*garib*', the poor who are always present in rural

Bangladesh. They are in the background of every scene, always there but seldom noticed as they watch village life on its margins. Not all of them beg, of course; only the most desperate and helpless are forced to tread that endless round. Others, like Ambia, who are just a little further from the edge of utter poverty, labour for their rice. It was these people who so often asked me, 'How can I do anything but work every day that I have? When your belly is empty, how can you think of anything else but earning rice to fill it with?'

Ambia, too, had said these words. And like the others, she had also taken my hand and put it between hers. That night, as I lay on my back and stared up at my net, listening to the rain and the crickets, it was this gesture which I thought of, and which for me summed up so much. She held my hand gently for a while, looking at it carefully, and then offered me her own. It was covered in callouses, and her nails were torn and black with the day's work.

'This is my hand,' she said. 'Are all the fingers on it of equal size? No, they're not. Some are big and strong, and others are small and weak. Allah never made fingers equal, and it's the same for people; everyone has their place. Some people are big, and others are small, like me. Everyone in your country is big ... You must tell your government to send money. And will you pray for me, Elder Sister?'

She stopped, and we both looked down at our hands. Mine: soft, white, and painted with Sufia's intricate henna designs – a hand quite obviously not accustomed to physical labour; and hers lying beside it: a rough and dirty hand, unpampered, uncared for, and just about to go back to work.

12 NOVEMBER – DEPARTURE

'If I have sinned against you, will you forgive me in the name of God?'

Old Janfu Ullah held his hand out to me with these, the formal words of goodbye, and smiled ruefully.

'You have never sinned against me, but I forgive you,' I replied. In three days I had visited almost every bari in the village, and I had my answers pat.

'Will you forget us?' everyone asked over those last weeks. 'Will you pray for us? Will you be married? Will you come back?'

And of course, the all-important: 'Who are you going to give your saris to?'

For months now, my possessions had been the subject of extreme speculation amongst the poorer villagers. Every sari, blouse and petticoat was earmarked, as well as my bedding, my by now filthy hurricane lamp and my grimy mosquito net. The redistribution had been a difficult task; torn clothes which would be thrown away in Britain were subjects of long discussion and dispute. Every day someone came to me to report: 'So-and-so says you promised your orange sari to her daughter, but didn't you promise it to me?' until I eventually refused to discuss the subject, and snapped only, 'I don't know! I never said anything to anybody!'

Eventually everything was doled out, with me hating my new role as benefactor and the lucky handful of friends who got a worn sari or aged hurricane lamp, relieved that as the fantastically rich Londoni I undoubtedly was, I had at last come up with the goods.

'Oh, Precious Ma,' one toothless old lady told me as she gripped my hand, 'now you have your own poor to care for, your own relatives'.

This declaration, although intended to please and flatter me, confirmed a situation which I had struggled to avoid all year – being seen as a patron; a local bigwig, with all the prestige and power – and all the obligations – that the dispensing of charity brought. But in those last weeks I had realised that if I really did want to think myself a true part of things, my qualms would have to be repressed. It was no good. I was rich, and loaded down with possessions which many people were quite prepared to nag me about for months, *ad nauseam*, and now was the time for me to play my part.

On my very last night in Talukpur, however, I paid the price of establishing myself as a Great Patron. A chill wind suddenly arrived to herald the new winter, and since I had given my blanket away I spent those final hours of darkness shivering in a borrowed sari and heartily cursing myself.

Giving away everything I had used in the village was only one part of the complex rites of my departure. In the last week Sufia hennaed my hands more elaborately than ever, and the family began to discuss who would accompany me to Sylhet. The weather had suddenly changed to clear days and cool nights, and I began to watch the fiery sunsets and shimmering dawns with something approaching nostalgia, as if I were already watching some aged cine film of 'my days in the village'. The fields were drying out once more. The flood waters had completely receded, and the family boats were again lying redundant in the mud and water hyacinths.

'Stay just a little longer, Katy,' people told me, 'and you'll see our land turn to gold and the time of harvest once more.'

The moon rose huge and pink over the pond and reminded me that it would be many days before I would sit under a Bengali sky again.

'You have become our blood,' Amma said one night, 'but now you must make yourself an English beti again. Why become like a Bangladeshi girl if you have to leave us? Why don't you marry here and stay?'

But this was not on the cards, and never had been. My transformation into a Bangladeshi woman had never been more than a surface veneer of habits and appearances which for the most part had remained entirely within my control. My hair was oiled, and I had learnt to walk and talk like the villagers, but inside my Western nature had remained intact, albeit with a few dents. I had for some time realised just how adaptable human nature is, and how easily it moulds itself to context. Rather like a dried-up sponge, I had soaked up behaviour and feelings whilst in the village, which were quickly squeezed out back in Dhaka, or amongst Western friends in Sylhet.

If strange men entered our bari I too would now leave and hide with the women, and I felt genuinely embarrassed and naked if a man came across me outside with my head uncovered. I loathed walking through the tea-stall area in the village, and if the trip was unavoidable I covered my head as much as possible with my umbrella, to shield it from male glances. I had begun to worry that sharom was contagious, and I had caught it. But this was hardly the case; instead, I had taken the parts of the purdah mentality which I found useful, rather than swallowing it whole. As a Western woman, however much she had 'become our blood', I was in a position of power to manipulate the system. I could take from purdah the 'freedom from' which it gives: a Muslim woman in Bangladesh, if she's lucky and her family can protect her, is free from the stares and pestering of men, or the trials of having to manage in the tough outside world, and at one level that can sometimes be very appealing. But where purdah threatened my 'freedom to', I was always able to reject it. If I was genuinely interested in talking to a male guest or walking to a nearby village alone, my feelings of sharom were easily overcome by a more rudimentary Western assumption of personal liberty.

The village had taught me things other than how to feel sharom. To my Western friends' horror, I had learnt not only how to burp and spit with the greatest of acumen, but also how to be incredibly rude. 'Go away! No, I'm not going to give you anything, leave me alone!' was something I now said with great ease to any unfortunate child or beggar who had come to me hoping for charity. Without realising it, I had got extremely used to being served by my junior brothers and sisters in the family, and like everyone else I now ordered: 'Give me my rice' when I was hungry, and took the food with a grunt. '*Dunudo bad*' (thank you) had only ever inspired laughter when I used it anyway. All in all, my polite English tact, ('Er ... I'm rather tired now ... ') had proved quite useless, and I had become, to say the least, direct. Outside the village I found myself doing things which somehow didn't seem quite right, although I had forgotten why. 'So, are you married? Do you have children?' I asked expatriates in Dhaka, or 'That's a nice wedding ring. How much did it cost?' Luckily I never asked anyone why they had spots, but probably came close to it. Western 'manners' and general politeness, it would seem, are attached to us by only the weakest of cultural glues, and fall away speedily once the setting no longer demands them. Conversely, I still feel uneasy if I eat, or hand something to someone, with my left hand.

Some habits die hard. The village dialect, for a start, with which I had struggled so painfully (and my rendition had never been flawless), was now quite ingrained. The posh Calcutta diction which I had been taught in London now sounded silly to me, and not half so melodious as Sylheti. But outside the village it did not go down well. 'Oh, Katy!' middle-class Bengali friends back in Dhaka cried when I tried to speak to them in my version of Bangla. 'Urgh! It's horrible! Why have you picked up such a dreadful way of speaking?'

More embarrassingly, some of the things I had learnt were downright insulting in Dhaka. 'O-Beti' ('Hey, lass!') was a little saying that I'd used quite happily all year, but in the capital an educated friend had to take me aside and tell me just how rude it was. I had also slipped into the habit of addressing all the women I met by the informal 'you', '*tumi*', rather than the honorific '*apni*', and they returned the compliment. Once again, in the town I realised all too late how insulting I was being. My use of 'tumi' appeared an imposition of higher status over the smart women I was meeting, who resolutely called me 'apni'. But worst of all, I referred to rickshaw drivers by the 'O-Beta' ('Hey, man!') which in the village had been a friendly, albeit rather familiar, way of attracting a man's attention. Only after I had been doing this on a regular basis every time I went to Dhaka did I learn that there, what I had thought to be an amiable little phrase translates roughly as 'Oi, shit-head'.

'But that's terrible!' I cried when I was told.

'Why do you worry?' the upper-class man I was talking to replied. 'It does not matter. They are rickshaw drivers. They are used to being called a shit-head.'

Language aside, other endearing little quirks seem to be here to stay. I still have to fight the urge to spit and burp loudly (and often fail), and back in London I find it hard not to drop down into a squatting position whenever I have to wait for a tube or bus. Of course, we take what we want from a culture we live in only temporarily, and then adapt back again. Like that henna on my hands, which was slowly to fade in the British cold, so did my Bengali-ness. Little by little, everything which I had thought so set was to slip away.

'Katy, tonight we shan't sleep, but talk until it is the time for dawn prayer again.'

I had found Sufia down at the ghat of Kudi Bibi's bari, her hands red from exertion as she pounded washing out on the stone steps. The day had been strange for me ever since I had woken to the now familiar sounds of Abba's prayers. I had been out since breakfast, paying my final visits and repeating again and again that I would write to the people of the village, that I could never forget them, and that no, I was not returning to Britain to marry a boy my parents had arranged for me.

'When you come back you must not be alone again,' countless people told me. 'Next time bring your husband, a new brother-in-law for us.'

The day I had so longed for, and so dreaded, had finally come. For me, the end of my life in the village was both a great release and a tragedy. Now I could return to where, I told myself, I truly belonged. I could stop being 'good' and conforming to rules which were basically so alien to me; I could be a free, Western woman again. Village life, on an everyday basis, is an extremely monotonous affair, and at times I had been excruciatingly bored. I often longed to escape; to speak my own language, and be with people from my own culture. My sixteen months in Bangladesh had at times also been extremely lonely.

The trips I took each month to Dhaka for a rest did little to help, for the luxuries of expatriate life there – swimming pools, parties, and huge air-conditioned houses with as much privacy as anyone could ever want – made it even harder to return to the village; anyway, I did not really belong there, either. It was Britain which in my most maudlin moments I yearned for, where nobody stared, or forced me to eat rice, or lectured me on religious matters. But even though I had at times wanted to stop playing my village role and become myself again, amongst my own friends and family, it was a role which I had also got very used to. After all those months, my village persona had become as much a part of me as that other, more complex and articulate one. As my knowledge of Bangla increased, and I became closer to people in the village, I became less lonely, too. After my initial struggles, living in Talukpur had become terribly easy; the wants and desires which are aroused by life in Britain simply did not exist. In so many ways my life was incredibly simple and pressure-free; even the monotony had become comforting in its predictability. And so without really noticing what was happening, I had stopped missing Britain, or even anyone there, and as the month of my departure grew near I realised in amazement that the thought of once more becoming an *Inreji beti*

(English girl) terrified me. Suppose I could no longer fit into Western life? Suppose I had become in some way warped by life in the village, a hopeless case of sharom and tactlessness? And of course there was my family in the village too, whom I had no idea when I would see again.

'We shall all eat our rice together, too,' Sufia continued as she wrung out a sari, and flicked it over her shoulder with a professionalism which I had never mastered. She had been telling me for weeks how on my last night in the village she would come and sleep in our household, so we could sit up late and talk. 'Come on, come inside with me, and I'll give you some of that special jorda my uncle brought from Sylhet.'

That night, for the last time, all the women in the household sat up and shared our secrets. No one felt like sleeping, and we talked long into the early hours as the wind blew through the betel trees outside and rattled the tin roof. I told the women, whom I had grown to love so much, many things about my life which I had previously held back, fearing that they could never understand and would be horrified by our Western ways. But they understood all right, and I only regretted my stupid assumptions, and that I had not shared these things with them earlier. For their part, the family told me what everyone had thought when I had first arrived.

'An agent from the British CIA!' they said. 'Ooh, we were so scared of you. But we know that's not true now, that you're good. What CIA person would stay with us for so long?'

Later, only Sufia and I were left. We sat on the verandah looking out at the dark yard.

'Whom shall I tell my griefs to when you're gone?' she whispered. 'Before, even though you sometimes went off to Sylhet and Dhaka, you were still with us. But now, however much I look for you across the fields, I'll know you won't be coming.'

'It will be OK,' I told her. Just you see. When I come back, you'll be happy and with a new baby.'

'If it is the will of Allah. But He wills me sadness. I can do nothing.'

Just as I tried to reassure her, Sufia told me how wonderful my life would be back in Britain. 'You'll marry a man with a great job, a university professor, and you'll take a job with a really high salary. You'll have lots of babies I'm sure.'

The spectre of hordes of babies and my 'university professor' did not fill me with the joy and excitement that perhaps it should have, but it did not matter. Neither of us truly understood the other's predicament, but the thought was there. At about 3 a.m., shivering slightly from the unaccustomed cool and aware that this was the last time we would sleep under the same roof, we went to bed.

'The boat has come! The boat has come!' the little boys of the bari screamed as they ran back from the river-bank. The bari had been full of people since early morning waiting to see me off, and now at last it was time to go. I had been wandering around in a state of semi-disbelief that I really was leaving.

'Will you forget our words?' everyone asked. 'What will you write about us back in London?'

I walked alone to the back of the bari and looked out across the fields for one last time. The rainy-season floods had begun to dry out now, and from the soggy morass the form of the land was once more reappearing. In another month it would be turning golden with the ripening paddy, fulfilling its yearly promise of new crops and restocking the family's grain stores. 'This isn't earth, but pure gold,' Abba had always said, his lined face creasing into smiles as he gestured towards his fields.

The beautiful land of Sylhet, enriched by the bones of its dead saints; the earth that exiled migrants living thousands of miles away in the West were flown back to be buried in, and which kept the villagers' bellies filled with rice – this land had been the constant backdrop to my life, with the views of its green paddy fields turning to gold, to baked brown, and then back to flood lands again. I wanted to take a clump of it away so I could have a little bit of Bangladesh with me always.

'What are you doing here all alone, Elder Sister?'

Banessa and Kudi Bibi were picking their way through the under-growth to where I was squatting.

'I'm looking at your beautiful fields,' I said.

'Are you crying, Elder Sister?'

Rather than a cause of shame, public tears are given the utmost social approbation, so instead of repressing them as I had done when I had left Britain a year and a half ago, I now gave them every encouragement.

'Am I crying? How can I not cry? And don't call me "Elder Sister", Banessa, we're equal.'

Banessa eyed me with knowing scepticism, and took my arm. 'Are you coming back? And when you come back, will you bring us all new saris, Elder Sister?'

Back in the bari buildings, Amma, Bebi and Ambia were preparing no end of delicacies to fill me up with. They had rather resentfully served the landless women who were sitting in my room with tea and betel nut, and quite clearly wished that they would all go and that I would stop forcing them to treat them like equals. There were so many people around that each room was full.

But now, it seemed that the little boys were right and the boat which would punt me through the water lilies back to the road really had arrived. It was time to go. Abba would come with me to Sylhet, with one of Amma's sisters and her children. There I would take my leave of them, and make my own way back to Dhaka. I shooed everyone out of my room, closed the door, and took off my sari, that long piece of cotton which had symbolised to me, more than anything else, my life in the village. 'Will you wear a sari in London?' the women had always asked me, and I had only ever replied that no, things were different there, it would not be appropriate. This was my own private ritual, unwinding the soft material and unbuttoning my thin blouse. In a week's time I would be swathed in jumpers and thermal underwear.

I reappeared in my shalwar kameez, and went around the large group of waiting people to hug them all, and touch their noses with mine. There was little Bebi, wiping her eyes with her grimy orna; Najma; Saleya clutching her baby; the Chairman's hand to shake; Kudi Bibi with her thin wiry body to hug; and many more of the people who had treated me with such unquestioning kindness. I did not hug Sufia or Amma until we were on the banks of the river. As was expected on such an occasion, we all cried ourselves silly. A tinsel garland was put over my head, and my bags were put in the painted cabin of the boat.

'I'll come back, I'll never forget you,' I told everyone.

'Yes,' they replied, 'but this time bring a husband'.

I had no words for Sufia. We both knew that our lives must now take us in separate directions, but that we would always love each other.

'Katy, send us photos.'

'Katy, pray for us!'

But I missed all the directions which were being shouted at me, for Rusheek, our Hindu boatman, had already pushed the boat off into the water, and we were slowly floating away into the centre of the river.

I could still see the group of people standing on the banks watching me go, when the boat turned a corner in the river and was carried by a sudden swell in the current, taken downstream and away from the scattered baris, until they were quite out of view.

GLOSSARY

abba/abazie: father
akika: naming ceremony for baby
amma/ammazie: mother
apni: you (honorific)
azan: call to prayer, broadcast from the mosque five times a day
babazie: father
babi: wife of elder brother, with whom one has a jokey, relaxed relationship
bangla-ghor: spare room for male guests, apart from the women
bari: homestead, a collection of households at one site, which are usually all of the same lineage
bedi: small, very cheap cigar
beta: man, bloke
betel: hard nut, chewed with spices and pan leaf
beti: woman, lass
bhut: evil spirits, ghosts
biriani: rice fried with meat, raisins and spices
burqua: cape which covers the whole body, with a veil for the face; worn by women in Muslim countries to hide themselves in public
da: long blade placed on the ground, for cutting
dada: father's father or father's uncle; senior man
datri: village midwife, usually an older woman
dhal: lentils
dular bhai: elder sister's husband
dunndo bad: thank you
eefta: food taken at the end of fasting, during Ramadan
Eid: Muslim festival. In Islam there are two Eids, the first after the month of fasting, Ramadan; and the second, Qurbani Eid, to commemorate the deaths of Mohammed's grandsons.

146

foo: blowing to heal, a common part of traditional healing in Bangladesh
fufu: father's sister
garib: the poor
ghat: area leading to water
Haj: pilgrimage to Mecca
henna: red dye made from crushed leaves, which women paint on their hands
holud: turmeric root, giving a yellow dye
hookah: long 'hubble-bubble' pipe for smoking tobacco, used by older men (and sometimes women)
jadhu: magic
jinni: Islamic spirit (plural: jinn)
jook: leech
jorda: sweetened tobacco chewed with betel and pan leaves
kabul: (Arabic) agreement
khala: mother's sister
kobiraj: traditional healer using herbal remedies and sometimes magic
Londoni: somebody who lives in Britain
lungi: cloth like a sarong, worn by men
madrasa: Islamic college, where students are taught Qur'anic verse, law and history
mama: mother's brother
mazaar: shrine
mehsahib: term of respect for person with religious knowledge; student at madrasa
misti: sweet/sweetmeat
mullah: Muslim priest, or man with Islamic learning
nani/nanazie: mother's mother or mother's aunt; senior woman
orna: long scarf worn across woman's bosom or head, with shalwar kameez (see below)
palki: death casket, for taking a body to the burial ground
pan: green spicy leaf, chewed with betel nut, spices and lime
panchayat: traditional village council, where cases are adjudicated
Patni: Hindu fisherman caste
pir: Muslim saint, holy man
pita: rice cakes, made with rice flour and steamed
pori: female spirit who possesses men
punjabi: men's traditional-style shirt
purdah: women's seclusion; the veil

Qur'an: Holy Book of Islam
Ramadan: Holy month of fasting in Islam
ruti: unleavened bread
saheb: term of respect
salaam: respectful greeting, often involving touching person's feet
salaam–e–lekum: Islamic greeting
sassa: father's brother
sassi: wife of father's brother
shalwar kameez: long baggy shirt and trousers, worn by young unmarried girls
sharom: shame
shwari: covered sedan chair traditionally used for carrying secluded women; now mostly used at weddings to carry brides to their husband's village
tabij: amulet, with Arabic or magical writings, wrapped into a tiny casket and attached to the body
taka: Bangladeshi currency; 1 taka = 2p (in 1988)
tumi: you (informal)
Vishnu: Hindu deity